BURT LANCASTER
THE MAN AND HIS MOVIES

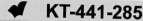

BURT LANCASTER
THE MAN AND HIS MOVIES

Allan Hunter

PAUL HARRIS PUBLISHING
Edinburgh

BY THE SAME AUTHOR

Alec Guinness on Screen
Local Hero: The Making of the Film (with Mark Astaire)
Walter Matthau (forthcoming)

First published in Great Britain 1984 by
Paul Harris Publishing (1976) Ltd.
40 York Place
Edinburgh

ISBN 0 86228 083 4

Typeset by Jo Kennedy, Edinburgh
Printed by Billings & Sons Ltd., Worcester

CONTENTS

Acknowledgements

A great deal of information was gleaned from newspapers, magazines and books. Although it is impossible to credit them all individually, the debt must be recorded.

A special thank you must also be expressed to the staff of the British Film Institute and National Film Archive for their unfailing efficiency and helpfulness in providing information and supplying all the photographs reproduced here.

I acknowledge the copyright retained by the film companies in reproducing their publicity photographs from the films of Burt Lancaster. Photographs are credited individually.

If anyone has not received full accreditation apologies are made here.

Allan Hunter.

THE MAN

Luchino Visconti, the Italian director, once described working with Burt Lancaster on *The Leopard*; 'The prince himself was a very complex character—at times romantic, good, understanding, sometimes even stupid and, above all, mysterious. Burt is all these things too. I sometimes think Burt is the most perfectly mysterious man I ever met in my life'.

Burt Lancaster the man remains somewhat enigmatic—a brawny acrobat who wound up a respected actor; a vulgar, hot-headed man who loves opera, ballet, paintings and fine literature; a perfectionist on set who can be unbending and flexible in equal measures; a quiet, introverted golfer with a con man's charm and bravura. At different times Burt Lancaster has displayed all these characteristics.

Burton Stephen Lancaster was born on 2 November 1913 at 209 East 106th Street in New York City, one of five children. His father James worked as a clerk in the post-office earning forty-eight dollars a week. Central Park was only five minutes away and his life-long appetite for a good book was nurtured at the library on 110th Street. His mother proved a dominant influence as he would later recall; 'She instilled in me concepts as strong as orthodox religion. Her edicts were; however poor you were you never lied, you never stole and you always stuck by a promise. I remembered it always because she made sure I would—by using her strong right arm. If I didn't honour these rules I could expect, and got, a cuff that hurt. Ma was such a determined lady. We weren't really poor as a family but we had to watch every penny. We never had enough clothing. People didn't then. You expected to be not quite warm enough in the winter. But you simply ran and ran to keep warm.'

The young Lancaster was an avid moviegoer with idols like Valentino and Fairbanks. When the *Mark of Zorro* played at the Atlas Theatre in his

7

neighbourhood during 1920 Lancaster was among the first in line to see the film and was vividly impressed by Fairbanks' feats of derring-do.

He attended Public School 83 and the DeWitt Clinton High School. He showed a distinct ability for athletics and began to train seriously with his friend Nick Cravat who lived two blocks away on 108th Street. His athletic prowess was to lead to a basketball scholarship to New York University where he commenced studies in 1929. His real ambition was to have been an opera singer and, as a boy, he had sung in the church choir. Aged eleven he had appeared on stage in a neighbourhood play and was impressive enough to attract the attention of a theatrical agent. Lancaster dismissed the idea of joining the profession as 'sissy'.

At New York University he excelled in basketball, boxing, baseball and gymnastics but soon tired of the routine of college life which he found dull. During his second year he left and looked up his old childhood friend Nick Cravat with the idea of forming a partnership and working up an act. They survived a disastrous audition, in which Lancaster allegedly ripped his tights, and were hired by the Kay Brothers Circus in Petersburg, Virginia for the princely wage of three dollars a week plus board. The duo, billing themselves as Lang and Cravat, spent almost a decade at work in vaudeville, circuses and carnivals, at one point working for the Ringling Brothers and commanding fifteen dollars a show on the Poli Vaudeville circuit. In 1935 Lancaster married fellow circus performer June Ernst, whose speciality act was horizontal bar tricks. Their union was short-lived and the couple parted on friendly terms the following year.

In 1941, whilst performing in St Louis, he injured his right hand and a badly infected finger was threatened with amputation unless he gave up acrobatics. The act of 'Lang and Cravat' decided to go their separate ways but their friendship endured and Cravat appeared in many Lancaster films over the next thirty years. With twenty dollars to his name Lancaster set off to find a job in Chicago, staying with some circus friends until he found employment. He was hired as a floorwalker in the lingerie department of Marshall Field's department store and was later promoted to the position of salesman in men's haberdashery. As with his days at college he found the regimented routine deadly dull and endured the job for all of six months. Briefly, he was then a fireman and an inspector with the Fulton Market Refrigeration Company. He then moved to New York and landed an interesting position with the Community Concerts Bureau at the CBS network. He was to travel and arrange advance bookings but, within a week, he was drafted into the army.

Private First-Class Lancaster spent three years in the 5th Army, special services branch, travelling with the troops to North Africa, Italy and Austria. With his performing background he spent most of the period directing and acting in revues including one called *Stars and Gripes*. Occasionally he was promoted to NCO but was soon demoted for acts of mild insubordination. In Italy he met USO. entertainer Norma Anderson, the widow of an army flyer with a son, James. They married in Yuma, Arizona on 28 December 1946. Lancaster named his first production company *Norma* after his wife and the couple had four children of their own—William born in 1947, Susan in 1949, Joanna in 1951 and Sighle in 1954.

During the summer of 1945 Lancaster returned to New York on a furlough to visit Norma and, with the luck of the gods on his side, received the lucky break that made him a star. Norma was working as a secretary to radio producer Ray Knight

'Lang and Cravat' (Nick Cravat)

Signing the contract with Harold Hecht

and, while ascending in the lift one day, he was spotted by Jack Mahlor. A telephone call explained that Mahlor was an associate of Irving Jacobs then casting a Broadway play, *A Sound of Hunting*, and Lancaster, a muscular six foot two with fair hair was considered physically ideal for the part of Sergeant Mooney. If he could act as good as he looked then the part was his. Lancaster auditioned at the Warwick Hotel and was immediately cast, his discharge papers from the army came through just seven hours before rehearsals began. The play tried out for two weeks in Philadelphia before commencing a disappointing three week run on Broadway. The effect on Lancaster's career however was incalculable; he more than impressed the critics and received no less than seven firm offers from the talent scouts of the major film studios who had made a point of seeing the show. The irony of the situation can't have escaped Lancaster; before the War, whilst appearing at the Orpheum Theatre in Los Angeles he had made the rounds of the studios and encountered rejection tempered with the advice that there was little interest in an acrobat lacking any acting experience. Now, facing the entreaties of those self-same studios, he was understandably reluctant to rush headlong into the standard seven year contract. Sam Levene, a fellow actor in *A Sound of Hunting*, introduced him to Harold Hecht, who was in the process of establishing himself as an independent agent. They met and Lancaster was impressed enough by Hecht to sign with him and thus begin a long and fruitful partnership. Explaining his decision Lancaster said; 'Harold said to me, "I'm an agent and know everybody. I have no people, you would be important to me. A little agent has to keep his people working." I figured he was levelling with me, so I signed with him.'

Lancaster and Hecht considered the seven Hollywood offers and decided to sign with Hal B. Wallis, a producer of some stature, then working from his own company base at Paramount Studios. Lancaster moved to Hollywood in January 1946 under the following conditions; Wallis paid him one hundred dollars a week whilst he was groomed for a screen test, ten thousand dollars if he passed the test (which he did) and then a weekly salary of one thousand two hundred and fifty dollars whilst employed. Wallis had attempted to gain an exclusive contract on Lancaster's services; characteristically the actor refused to be tied down and the two agreed on a contract obligating Lancaster to two films a year for Wallis over the next seven years, with the options of making one film per annum for another company. Wallis gave him his first assignment – a major rôle in *Desert Fury* which was scheduled to go before the cameras in August. Lancaster, however, grew restless waiting and, deciding to start as he meant to continue, chose to exercise his option and work on an outside production.

Mark Hellinger, an independent producer at Universal, was then casting his film of the Hemingway short story *The Killers*; a key rôle of the ex-boxer, known as the Swede, remained unfilled. Lancaster managed to arrange for Hellinger to see his screen test and, suitably impressed, Hellinger agreed to meet the actor and, charmed into thinking he had discovered the ideal person for the part, signed him as the Swede. *The Killers* went into production in May and was completed before Lancaster was scheduled to begin work on *Desert Fury*. When *The Killers* was released, and with the aid of a studio campaign, Lancaster was hailed as a star and, overnight, catapulted into the front ranks of Hollywood leading men. One would not have expected a similar reaction had *Desert Fury* been his introduction to critics and filmgoers.

In Hollywood Lancaster remained essentially a family man and was little seen on the social circuit. At work he shrewdly began engineering the broadening of his career. Hellinger sought him for the brutal prison drama *Brute Force* whilst Wallis planned a gangster picture teaming him with Kirk Douglas. Lancaster could already see himself being typecast in action rôles and saw no long term prospects in this area. At work he could often be hot-headed and gained a reputation for telling directors what to do. As early as *I Walk Alone* he was arguing with Wallis about his salary. He needed all his charm to persuade Wallis to allow him to play the second lead in Arthur Miller's *All My Sons*. Choosy about scripts he turned down *Winter Meeting* although his co-star would have been Bette Davis. In 1948, probably to no-one's surprise, he incorporated and formed his own company – Norma Productions. He joined forces with Harold Hecht and, borrowing money, went into business with Universal Pictures. One of the first truly independent actor-owned production companies, Norma would set the film world on a trend which would ensure the break-up of the old studio system. Later in the company's history Lancaster would say; 'Hecht and I complement each other, Harold is the best executive I ever saw and an exceptional critic. He's not creative but infallible when it comes to knowing what's good. Jim Hill, our story man, is wonderful. And let me tell you, good material is the life and breath of this business. No actor can make a bad story good.' Lancaster's professional instincts have always been drawn to a good script and a director of integrity, regardless of the size of his billing or the number of lines that his character is assigned. He has often given of his vast experience and considerable box-office value for little financial remuneration. Conversely, there are pictures, like *Airport* and *The Cassandra Crossing* which he admits to making strictly for the money and to keep his name before the fickle public.

Amongst the first projects announced by Norma Productions was *Advance Man*, a film about a circus press agent whose job is to travel in advance of the show and arrange bookings. The script, by Lancaster himself, was never filmed, but the desire to make a circus picture persisted; ideal for Cecil B. De Mille's *The Greatest Show on Earth*, Warner Brothers refused to let him work at Paramount and the part of the trapeze artist fell to Cornel Wilde (back injuries had prevented Lancaster from appearing in De Mille's previous film *Samson and Delilah*). In 1956 Lancaster finally made his circus film, having paid one hundred thousand dollars for the script of *Trapeze*.

Norma-Hecht Productions began inauspiciously with *Kiss the Blood off my Hands*. However, when Lancaster put his former acrobatic skills into service they hit the jackpot. *The Flame and the Arrow*, a grand, old-style swashbuckler reviving the 'Lang and Cravat' partnership was a notable box-office success and the tongue-in-cheek vein continued in the Foreign Legion romp *Ten Tall Men* and the spoof *Crimson Pirate*. He was soon dubbed 'Mr Muscles and Teeth' and, equally quickly labelled as 'beefcake'. This image was immensely popular with the public and he twice appeared in the list of the top ten box-office stars in 1956 and 1962. Lancaster was rarely satisfied with his he-man image and his outside commitments at this point sought to give fuller rein to his dramatic talents and included the character rôle of the dipsomaniac Doc Delaney in *Come Back, Little Sheba* and the sergeant in *From Here to Eternity*. Throughout the fifties Lancaster's career boomed with only an occasional setback – his one attempt at direction, *The Kentuckian* was a failure. Nonetheless he reflected on the experience thus; 'I never worked so hard in my life. I was up at five o'clock every morning, and never got to bed before midnight. A director's job is unquestionaly the most demanding in the film. You are married to your work. You're not only the first one on the set but you work all day long, you make all the decisions, you deal with temperamental actors and actresses. Then the next day you start the same grind all over again. But it's the best job in pictures because when you're a director you are God. And, you know, that's the best job in town.'

He gained the reputation for totally dominating a production and Kirk Douglas commented; 'There's only one man worse than me for telling directors what to do, and that's Burt.' However, on the set of *From Here to Eternity* he met his match in co-star Montgomery Clift and admitted; 'The only time I was ever really afraid as an actor was that first scene with Clift. It was my scene understand: I was the sergeant, I gave the orders, he was just a private under me. Well, when we started, I couldn't stop my knees from shaking. I thought they might have to stop because my trembling would show. But I'd never worked with an actor with Clift's power before; I was afraid he was going to blow me right off the screen.' Both actors were nominated for the Academy Award as Best Actor of 1953.

With the addition of a third partner, James Hill, Hecht-Hill-Lancaster entered their most successful stage of operation and produced films in which Lancaster did not star including *The Bachelor Party* and *Summer of the Seventeenth Doll*. One surprise hit which met with much initial resistance was *Marty*, as Lancaster outlined; 'United Artists did not want us to do *Marty*. The budget was 250,000 dollars – it eventually cost 330,000 dollars. While we were shooting *Vera Cruz*, they came up to me and said, "We don't want you to do *Marty*." And I said, "Well fine, if you don't want us to do *Marty* then I don't want to work for you people any more. I think it is your responsibility to encourage films of this nature. The price of the film is small enough that you really cannot get hurt very badly, but you've got to encourage film-makers with new ideas, new talent." They finally gave in. They felt I was a marketable star and they wanted to keep my favour. We did *Marty*. But they were able to prove, incidentally, that a film like *Vera Cruz* which was made for 1,700,000 dollars, grossed 11 million, and *Marty* which cost 330,000 dollars grossed 5½ million. From their point of view, they had lost.'

Marty also garnered the prestige of winning the Oscar for the Best Film of 1955 with Ernest Borgnine being chosen as the Best Actor for his study of a Bronx butcher.

By 1958, Lancaster was a very wealthy and successful man, his name on a film costing 750,000 dollars plus 10 per cent of the profits. He confessed to a personal fortune of 3½ million dollars and was still much in demand throughout Hollywood. 20th Century Fox sought Cary Grant as Caesar with Lancaster as Anthony to Elizabeth Taylor's *Cleopatra* and he rejected *Ben Hur* because 'I disliked the approach to Christianity, I thought it cheapened it.' He did, however, find the part of itinerant con man Elmer Gantry made to measure and the resulting public and critical approval was gratifying. Nominated for a second time for the Oscar he was announced as the winner at a ceremony in April 1961 at the Santa Monica Civic Auditorium. He must have been particularly pleased as his co-nominees had included Laurence Olivier and Spencer Tracy, two artists he held in high esteem.

With the comfort of commercial success and a Best Actor Academy Award, the hot-tempered, ambitious young Lancaster of old had nothing left to prove. Perhaps the realisation of this coloured his choice of material in the sixties, a decade in which he strove to extend himself as an actor and examine the non-physical side of his character. It was a policy which brought mixed results; a further Oscar nomination for *Bird Man of Alcatraz* and his powerful count in *The Leopard*, two of his personal favourites, but also a string of box-office failures in *The Swimmer*, *Castle Keep* and *The Gypsy Moths*. In 1964 he told an interviewer; 'I just don't want to do anything else. I have all the money I shall ever need. The pleasure now is not in making the money but in doing what you want. I've always tried to do different things, things I wasn't even sure I could do. I feel an actor must do the things which interest him because its only way he will be able to give something of himself to the part.'

Hecht-Hill-Lancaster was wound up in the early sixties. Hecht had attempted, in vain, to dissuade Lancaster from a course of uncommercial stories which had begun with *Sweet Smell of Success* and continued through *The Devil's Disciple* to *Bird Man of Alcatraz*. The company ended heavily in debt.

Lancaster's perfectionist loyalty to a production is by now legendary and tales of arguments with actors and directors legion. Less well publicised have been his less star-like qualities of a cavalier attitude to whether his pictures make money and his persistance in encouraging new talent. In 1956 Tony Curtis found himself in a situation not unfamiliar to Lancaster of being a handsome movie idol convinced of his worth as a dramatic actor but relatively powerless to showcase his Thespian talents. Lancaster was impressed by his dedication to *Trapeze* and cast him against type as the unscrupulous press agent in *Sweet Smell of Success*. Lancaster encouraged the early career of Telly Savalas and promoted directors Sydney Pollack and John Frankenheimer. After their first film together Frankenheimer observed; 'I think that he is one of the most hard-working individuals I've ever met. He's a true professional. He cares deeply about what he does. He's very considerate of other actors. I think he's one of the few men, one of the few actors that I've met, who really knows something about production. He knows something about cutting, about the problems of making a film. I find it easy

Lancaster in his Oscar winning role as Elmer Gantry

to work with him. When he's been correctly cast, there is nobody better.' Also less publicised has been his unwavering liberalism and active participation in the Civil Rights Movement of the sixties. A staunch Democrat, he was a Kennedy man in the sixties and a McGovern supporter in 1972. He was a supporter too of Martin Luther King and in 1969 flew from a European film location for a one day involvement with the March on Washington. In Los Angeles he campaigned for Thomas Bradley who became the first black mayor of the city. His strong social conscience has often been reflected in his choice of screen material – *A Child is Waiting* looked at society's attitude to retarded children and *The Scalphunters* was an elegantly packaged plea for racial harmony.

In 1971 he achieved one of his long-standing ambitions and appeared at the Curran Theatre in San Fransisco in a stage production of *Knickerbocker Holiday*. Singing 'September Song' he received good notices and revealed a pleasant baritone voice, it was some compensation for never having made the grade as an opera-singer. His musical pursuits had never proved entirely fruitful; he once spent three months in vain trying to learn the piano. On his lost career as an opera-singer he lamented; 'The voice broke and I've spent the rest of my life searching for it.' At one point before the War he had picked up some rent money as a singing waiter in New Jersey.

In 1969 he had been divorced from Norma after twenty-three years of marriage. Norma had sued on grounds of cruelty and the marriage was believed to have foundered on Lancaster's compulsion with work to the detriment of his private life. It was further believed that a million dollar settlement was agreed upon although neither Norma nor Lancaster would discuss the split in public.

Lancaster's box-office status was not what it had once been when the film industry entered upon a periodic crisis during the early seventies. Lancaster, approaching sixty, found the quality of the material offered to him was generally inferior and he commented nostalgically on his independent successes of the fifties as: 'fun days when we set the town on fire with every movie we did.' In 1971 it was reported in *Playboy* that Lancaster and Kirk Douglas were unbankable for any film costing over two million dollars. He turned to the traditional refuge of ageing stars and made a trio of Westerns and a spy thriller, *Scorpio*, observing; 'It's character parts from now on. I'd look rather silly making love to a nineteen-year-old girl.'

After the failure of his second attempt at direction, *The Midnight Man*, it was assumed he might retire and he did claim he would appreciate the time to take up cooking, gardening, indulge his passion for opera and golf, whilst relaxing with his constant companion Jackie Bone, his former secretary. His family were all grown up, his son William entering his father's profession most notably with the script for *The Bad News Bears* in 1976. His days as a provider for seven were long over. However, there was an occasional challenge – a reunion with Visconti on *Conversation Piece* and a rôle for Bertolucci in *1900*. Co-workers found him as meticulous as ever and a shade mellower, reflecting his age. At the time of *Atlantic City* he hadn't been stretched as an actor in years. A series of efficient performances in a variety of globe-scattered locations had never disappointed audiences but the forceful, versatile Lancaster of old had been somewhat subdued. He had been unable to elicit much response for several personal projects including *Son of the Crimson Pirate* or *Draws*, a light Western with Kirk Douglas as his projected co-star. A biography of Robert E. Lee for Roger Corman remained at the planning stage and a villainous rôle in *The Legend of the Lone Ranger* never came to pass.

Atlantic City re-affirmed his reputation as a gifted actor and brought an armful of awards which he welcomed in the hope that they might create an audience for the picture. When the Los Angeles Film Critics voted him Best Actor he stated; 'Maybe the award will help, for apart from myself, Kirk Douglas and my immediate family I don't think anyone has seen the picture.' The film also revitalised his career to an extent and, at seventy, Lancaster is once again in demand for an interesting range of scripts. He has been quick to seize the new opportunity of his autumnal years, unsuccessful in seeking a rôle in *Gorky Park* but filming extensively in Italy, journeying to Scotland, undertaking a stage play in Los Angeles with Kirk Douglas and, back on his old stomping ground, on a movie set in America, filming *The Osterman Weekend*, his first film with Sam Peckinpah. In 1980 he was on the critical list after an eleven hour operation for an undisclosed abdominal condition, it was emphasised that he was not suffering from cancer and the energy which he has displayed over the past three years has put paid to any such fears.

Burt Lancaster – the man, is compulsive, dedicated, loyal and a perfectionist. Jeanne Moreau, his co-star in *The Train*, once remarked; 'Before he can pick up

Off set during the filming of *Ten Tall Men* 1951

Discussion with director Bill Forsyth during the filming of *Local Hero* 1982

an ashtray, he discusses his motivation for an hour or two. You want to say, just pick up the ashtray and shut up!' Over nearly four decades of stardom Lancaster has remained true to his own code of manners, behaviour and priorities. He has balanced his career between the commonsense approach of realising the need to remain a viable commercial property whilst acknowledging that if stardom means nothing else it means the luxury of risk-taking by following personal instincts. He raised his children away from the publicity glare of Hollywood life and the camera, and rarely compromised on the important issues. Not unexpectedly it is the Lancaster integrity passed on from his mother which shines through; he has refused to make commercials and only tolerates the drawbacks of stardom to enjoy the rewards. He once explained; 'People outside Hollywood don't understand how it is here. It's a battle to maintain a basic integrity, a scrap against bull and baloney. You have to fight all the time.'

In 1968 he was quoted in an interview as saying; 'As an actor I know I can still improve. Oh God, yes, we've all got to keep trying to reach new horizons.' It is a characteristic remark. Lancaster has been amongst the most forward-looking actors of his generation, always restless for new challenges and new horizons – in production or direction or acting, in Europe or America. Age shows no sign of quenching his ambition or stilling his desire to perform. After sixty-seven major film rôles, an Oscar, box-office success and criticai acclaim he summed up four decades of personal development recently; 'As you get older you have to keep your mind open. I feel you must also try new things. Some of us learn finally that maturity means consideration for other people. I think it is the ability to love yourself and consequently others. That is the answer. I know now it is not necessary to go through life being a warrior.'

THE MOVIES

1946: *The Killers*
1947: *Desert Fury*
   : *Brute Force*
   : *I Walk Alone*
1948: *All My Sons*
   : *Sorry, Wrong Number*
   : *Kiss the Blood off My Hands*
1949: *Criss Cross*
   : *Rope of Sand*
1950: *The Flame and the Arrow*
   : *Mister 880*
1951: *Vengeance Valley*
   : *Jim Thorpe – All American*
   : *Ten Tall Men*
1952: *The Crimson Pirate*
   : *Come Back Little Sheba*
1953: *South Sea Woman*
   : *From Here to Eternity*
   : *His Majesty O'Keefe*
1954: *Apache*
   : *Vera Cruz*
1955: *The Kentuckian*
   : *The Rose Tattoo*
1956: *Trapeze*
   : *The Rainmaker*
1957: *Gunfight at the O.K. Corral*
   : *Sweet Smell of Success*
1958: *Run Silent, Run Deep*
   : *Separate Tables*
1959: *The Devil's Disciple*
1960: *The Unforgiven*
   : *Elmer Gantry*
1961: *The Young Savages*
   : *Judgement at Nuremberg*
1962: *Birdman of Alcatraz*
   : *A Child is Waiting*
   : *The Leopard*
1963: *Seven Days in May*
1964: *The Train*
1965: *The Hallelujah Trail*

1966: *The Professionals*
1968: *The Swimmer*
   : *The Scalphunters*
1969: *Castle Keep*
   : *The Gypsy Moths*
   : *Airport*
1970: *Valdez is Coming*
   : *Lawman*
1972: *Ulzana's Raid*
   : *Scorpio*
1973: *Executive Action*
1974: *The Midnight Man*
   : *The Conversation Piece*
1975: *Moses*
   : *1900*
1976: *Buffalo Bill and the Indians*
   : *The Cassandra Crossing*
   : *Victory at Entebbe*
1977: *Twilight's Last Gleaming*
   : *The Island of Dr Moreau*
1978: *Go Tell the Spartans*
1979: *Zulu Dawn*
1980: *Cattle Annie and Little Britches*
   : *Atlantic City, USA*
1981: *The Skin*
1983: *Local Hero*
   : *The Osterman Weekend*

OTHERS

1947: *Variety Girl* (guest)
1953: *Three Girls and a Sailor* (guest)
1957: *Playtime in Hollywood* (short)
1963: *The List of Adrian Messenger* (cameo)
1969: *King: A Filmed Record . . . Montgomery to Memphis* (documentary)
1976: *The Cinema According to Bertolucci* (documentary)

THE KILLERS

(USA 1946)

RUNNING TIME: 105 minutes

Mark Hellinger Productions for Universal Pictures

CAST: Edmond O'Brien (Jim Reardon), Ava Gardner (Kitty Collins), Albert Dekker (Big Jim Colfax), Sam Levene (Lt. Sam Lubinsky), Burt Lancaster (Swede), Charles McGraw (Al), William Conrad (Max), Jack Lambert (Dum Dum), Jeff Corey (Blinky)

DIRECTOR: Robert Siodmak
PRODUCER: Mark Hellinger
ASSOCIATE PRODUCER: Jules Buck
SCREENPLAY: Anthony Veiller from the story by Ernest Hemingway.
ART DIRECTORS: Jack Otterson and Martin Obzina
DIRECTOR OF PHOTOGRAPHY: Elwood Bredell
EDITOR: Arthur Hilton
SOUND: Bernard B. Brown
MUSIC: Miklos Rozsa
COSTUMES: Vera West

PLOT SYNOPSIS:

In the small town of Brentwood, Peter Lunn, known as the Swede, works as a filling station attendant fatalistically awaiting his death at the hands of two hired killers. Through flashbacks we learn of his involvement with glamorous singer Kitty Collins on whose behalf he has served time. Six years previously, together with Kitty, her lover Colfax, Blinky and Dum Dum he had carried out the Prentice Hat robbery, netting $254,912. Warned by Kitty of an impending double-cross the Swede deceived the other gang members, departing with Kitty and all the money. Two days later, in Atlantic City, Kitty left the Swede high and dry without funds. Disillusioned, the Swede awaits the inevitable retribution of the gang.

When the Swede is murdered Blinky and Dum Dum (unaware of Kitty's involvement) are alerted to his whereabouts and head for Brentwood in search of the money.

The beneficiary of the Swede's $2500 life insurance policy is a maid at a hotel in Atlantic City. Insurance investigator Reardon suspects a link with the Prentice Hat robbery and, together with police lieutenant Lubinsky, sets out to solve the case. Blinky is shot, confessing details of the robbery before his death. Piecing the case together Reardon tracks down Kitty Collins. Kitty now claims to be happily married and admits to double-crossing the Swede and taking the money. In the bar where they meet there is a shoot-out with the hired killers and Kitty gives the authorities the slip. She is traced to Colfax's house. He is her husband and together they had cheated everyone. In crossfire with the police Dum Dum and Colfax are killed, with the latter refusing to clear Kitty with an all-embracing death bed confession. The six year old case has been solved.

(Photo: Mark Hellinger Productions) Ava Gardner

COMMENT:

Although not scheduled as his first film, *The Killers* was made and distributed before Lancaster went to work on his commitments for Hal Wallis and thus constitutes his screen début. Ernest Hemingway's short story originally appeared in *Scribner's* magazine in 1927 and John Huston is believed to have been involved in adapting the story into a screenplay.

For the rôle of the Swede, a lumbering former boxer, Mark Hellinger had sought the services of Wayne Morris, who had recently returned from war service to re-commence his film contract at Warner Brothers. Warner Brothers asked seventy-five thousand dollars for the use of Morris which Hellinger politely refused. He had also considered Sonny Tufts for the part but remained dubious as to the latter's acting ability. Once Lancaster had made himself known to Hellinger, he was cast in the part and *The Killers* filmed in Hollywood from May to July 1946.

'it's a gangster yarn and it starts off with the murder, in cold blood, of a nice, big, handsome newcomer to the screen, Burt Lancaster.'

Sunday Dispatch

'Burt Lancaster plays the Swede and you won't forget his performance.'

Daily Graphic

'Burt Lancaster, who plays the ex-boxer, may well be a new star.'

Sunday Express

DESERT FURY

(USA 1947)

RUNNING TIME: 96 minutes

Hal Wallis Production

CAST: Lizabeth Scott (Paula Heller), John Hodiak (Eddie Bendix), Burt Lancaster (Tom Hanson), Mary Astor (Fritzi), Wendell Corey (Johnny), James Flavin (Pat Johnson), William Harrigan (Berle Lindquist), Kristine Miller (Claire Lindquist), Jane Novak (Mrs Lindquist)

DIRECTOR: Lewis Allen
PRODUCER: Hal B. Wallis
SCREENPLAY: Robert Rossen
ART DIRECTOR: Perry Ferguson
DIRECTORS OF PHOTOGRAPHY: Charles Lang and Edward Cronjager
MUSIC: Miklos Rozsa

PLOT SYNOPSIS:

Chuckawalla, a desert gambling city. Attractive Paula Heller returns home for good to her mother Fritzi, the wealthy owner of a large gambling saloon. Very soon she is infatuated with slick, crooked gambler Eddie Bendix. She is warned of his unsavoury character by both Fritzi and her friend Tom Hanson, the local deputy-sheriff. However, the two carry on an illicit affair.

Eddie's partner Johnny is increasingly resentful of Paula's intrusion in Eddie's affairs and her growing influence over him. Johnny decides to create trouble by informing Fritzi of their relationship however, Eddie demands that he be allowed to marry Paula. Fritzi tells Paula of Eddie's life, of his underhand dealings and how he is believed to have caused the death of his first wife by forcing her car off a bridge. Paula is blind to his faults and the two decide to leave town together.

On their way they stop to give a lift to Johnny despite the fact that his association with Eddie is now at an end. Later, at a wayside café, Johnny finally opens Paula's eyes to the real nature of Eddie Bendix. She takes off on her own but Eddie shoots Johnny and races after her in his car. Help is at hand when policeman Tom joins the chase and eventually Eddie's car crashes over the very same bridge on which he had forced his wife to her death. Eddie is killed and Laura is united with Tom who has always cared for her.

COMMENT:

Lancaster's part in *Desert Fury*, his first part for Hal Wallis, was not strong enough to help him realise his potential as star material. Concerned with developing Lancaster's career, Wallis was shrewd enough to delay the release of the picture until both *The Killers* and *Brute Force* had reached cinema audiences.

Desert Fury was filmed over a period of seventy-two days at Sedona in northern Arizona. The rugged locations included the Navajo Reservation, north of Flagstaff, and the small mining settlements of Cottonwood and Clarkdale. With Lancaster's growing screen image as a man of action, *Desert Fury* marked his first time ever on a horse.

Lizabeth Scott *(Photo: Hal Wallis Production)*

When the film was finally released most of the critics wondered exactly what all the fury was about although Mary Astor's bristling Fritzi was a welcome change from her series of mother rôles at MGM.

'It is a harsh, hard-bitten but handsome picture, ringing with the sounds of faces well slapped and jaws truly clipped.'

Daily Mail

'The acting is first-class. But except for Mr Lancaster as a speed cop, the characters in the Arizona town, with their lavish clothes and luxury roadsters, are contemptible to the point of being more than slightly nauseating.'

Daily Herald

BRUTE FORCE

(USA 1947)

RUNNING TIME: 96 minutes

Universal International Pictures

CAST: Burt Lancaster (Joe Collins), Hume Cronyn (Captain Munsey), Yvonne De Carlo (Gina), Ann Blyth (Ruth), Charles Bickford (Gallagher), Whit Bissell (Tom Lister), Sam Levene (Louie), John Hoyt (Spencer), Ella Raines (Cora), Anita Coley (Flossie)

DIRECTOR: Jules Dassin
PRODUCER: Mark Hellinger
ASSOCIATE PRODUCER: Jules Buck
SCREENPLAY: Richard Brooks from a story by Robert Patterson
ART DIRECTORS: Bernard Herzbrun and John F. De Cuir
DIRECTOR OF PHOTOGRAPHY: William Daniels
EDITOR: Edward Curtiss
SOUND: Charles Felstead and Robert Pritchard
MUSIC: Miklos Rozsa
COSTUMES: Rosemary Odell

PLOT SYNOPSIS:
Cell R17, Westgate Penitentiary. The inmates, led by small-time crook Joe Collins, ponder their private and home lives whilst suffering the stark contrast of the daily grind of a brutal prison existence. The prison is dominated by Captain Munsey, a sadistic officer with a passion for the music of Wagner, who taunts the prisoners for his own delight and foments trouble amongst the men to discredit his superior, the warden.

Collins is desperate to break out of the penitentiary as his young wife Ruth is ill and is reluctant to go through with an operation unless Joe can be with her. Collins enlists the aid of Gallagher, who runs the prison newspaper, and together they plan the escape from their block. Munsey hears of their plans but an informer is savagely killed before the full details are known.

The alcoholic prison doctor warns Collins and the men of the foolhardiness of their plans but to little avail. Collins, Gallagher and the others escape but Captain Munsey is lying in wait with machine-guns at the ready. All the men are killed but not before Collins has an opportunity to attack Munsey. In their struggle Munsey is thrown from the watch tower wall and plummets to his death. Joe is also killed.

COMMENT:
Before filming *Brute Force* Lancaster had made a guest appearance with Lizabeth Scott in the all-star Paramount feature *Variety Girl*. *Brute Force* reunited him with producer Mark Hellinger.

Hellinger, in his brief post-war career, sought to inject more social realism and maturity into the treatment of his favourite themes – crime and the underworld. Hellingers' productions, like *Brute Force* and *The Naked City*, embody what

28

Charles Bickford *(Photo: Universal International Pictures)*

were only later to become clichés – location shooting, clipped narrative and an unstinting depiction of violence. The brutality of *Brute Force*, although tame by present standards, was quite shocking to some movie audiences in 1947.

The scriptwriter on *Brute Force* was Richard Brooks, at this early stage he had in mind a film version of the 1927 book *Elmer Gantry* with Lancaster in the lead. It would be a further thirteen years before his plans came to fruition.

'The characterisation is firmly drawn, a quality which is shown to good advantage by a large cast headed by Burt Lancaster as Joe and by Hume Cronyn as the loathsome Munsey – both forceful and clever portrayals.'

Monthly Film Bulletin

I WALK ALONE

(USA 1947)

RUNNING TIME: 98 minutes

Hal Wallis Production

CAST: Burt Lancaster (Frankie Madison), Lizabeth Scott (Kay Lawrence), Kirk
   Douglas (Noll Turner), Wendell Corey (Dave), Kristine Miller (Mrs
   Richardson), George Rigaud (Maurice), Marc Lawrence (Nick Palestro),
   Mike Mazurki (Dan), Mickey Knox (Skinner), Roger Neury (Felix)

DIRECTOR: Byron Haskin
PRODUCER: Hal B. Wallis
SCREENPLAY: Charles Schnee from the play *Beggars are Coming to Town* by
   Theodore Reeves.
ART DIRECTORS: Hans Dreir and Franz Bachelin
DIRECTOR OF PHOTOGRAPHY: Leo Tover
MUSIC: Victor Young
COSTUMES: Edith Head

PLOT SYNOPSIS:

1947. Frankie Madison is released from prison after serving a fourteen year
sentence for rum-running during the era of Prohibition. He had taken the rap for
his partner Noll Turner and now expects to be compensated in full with a half
share in the empire which Noll has built over the ensuing years. Noll is now an
established force in racketeering with a sophisticated nightclub serving as his
legitimate business. Noll has no intention of sharing anything with Frankie and
uses vocalist Kay Lawrence to find out his ex-partner's intentions.

When Kay discovers that she is being cheaply exploited by Noll she changes
sides and joins forces with Frankie although the latter is powerless to intercede
in Noll's slickly operated organisation. Noll's financial guru, Dave, is repelled
by the violence Noll plans to use in disposing of Frankie and threatens to reveal
irregularites in the accounts. He is murdered and it seems that Noll will
successfully implicate Frankie in the slaying, thus dispensing with two
problems. However, Frankie, using the more familiar strong-arm tactics of his
trade, forces Noll to confess to the murder and, with Kay in tow, assumes
control of the Noll empire.

COMMENT:

I Walk Alone is now only notable for the first appearance together of Lancaster
and Kirk Douglas. Douglas had also been spotted on the New York stage by Hal
Wallis and signed to a contract for five pictures. Like Lancaster, he was adept at
manoeuvring his way through the Hollywood system and, after two Wallis films,
The Strange Love of Martha Ivers and *I Walk Alone*, he managed to break the
contract.

The fact that the play *The Beggars are Coming to Town* was a failure on
Broadway didn't deter Wallis from making this film version and building up his

(Photo: Hal Wallis Production) Kirk Douglas and Lizabeth Scott

Desert Fury team of Lancaster and Lizabeth Scott. It is interesting to note the low regard in which Lancaster was held as an actor at this time. The critics reaction to his work can only have intensified his desire to improve himself.

'Burt Lancaster plays with all the blank-faced aplomb of Tarzan.'
New York Times

'The peculiar gift of Burt Lancaster is that he can go on registering self-pity for an hour and a half without moving anything except his nostrils.'
Daily Mail

'This is one of the fastest, smoothest and most exciting thrillers for a long time with superb performances from Kirk Douglas, Wendell Corey and Burt Lancaster as the simple tough who cannot adjust himself to a world in which his strong-arm methods have gone somewhat out of fashion.'
Monthly Film Bulletin

ALL MY SONS

(USA 1948)

RUNNING TIME: 94 minutes

Universal International Pictures

CAST: Edward G. Robinson (Joe Keller), Burt Lancaster (Chris Keller), Mady Christians (Kate Keller), Louisa Horton (Ann Deever), Howard Duff (George Deever), Frank Conroy (Henry Deever), Lloyd Gough (Jim Bayliss), Arlene Francis (Sue Bayliss), Henry Morgan (Frank Lubey)

DIRECTOR: Irving Reis
PRODUCER: Chester Erskine
SCREENPLAY: Chester Erskine from the play by Arthur Miller
ART DIRECTORS: Bernard Herzbrun and Hilyard Brown
DIRECTOR OF PHOTOGRAPHY: Russell Metty
EDITOR: Ralph Dawson
SOUND: Leslie L. Carey and Carson Jowett
MUSIC: Leith Stevens
COSTUMES: Grace Houston

PLOT SYNOPSIS:

Joe Keller is an apparently successful small business man and generous family provider. However, during the recent war he has knowingly allowed his company to ship faulty airplane parts because he was desperate for the money. He believed that he was doing the best for his wife and children. Twenty-one airmen are killed because of Keller's negligence, including his own son Larry.

After the war the incident is investigated but Keller is acquitted through a legal technicality. The responsibility for the deaths is placed on his partner Henry Deever, who is imprisoned. Keller's other son, Chris, returns from his war service and falls in love with Ann, Deever's daughter. He visits Deever in prison and learns the truth of what has happened. Despite his respect and affection for his father Chris believes it imperative that Joe is made to realise the gravity of his actions. Chris produces a letter from his dead brother Larry which indicates that he knew of the defective parts and had deliberately flown to his death to atone for his shame.

Joe is grief-stricken by this information and realises symbolically that the twenty-one men killed were all his sons. Joe commits suicide and, the family guilt having been expiated, Chris feels free to court Ann with a clear conscience.

COMMENT:

Arthur Miller's *All My Sons*, the winner of the 1947 New York Drama Critics Circle Award, had been a Broadway success running for nine months. Lancaster was set on playing Chris Keller and it marks the first of many occasions on which he took a cut in pay to appear in a project he considered worthwhile. In an interview he said; 'I wanted to play Chris Keller because he had the courage to make his father realise that he was just as responsible for the deaths of many

Edward G. Robinson *(Photo: Universal International Pictures)*

servicemen as if he had murdered them. And, as I had been in the army, I had no difficulty in duplicating Chris's feelings. I believe that each person shares a responsibility for the welfare of others.'

In his autobiography, *All My Yesterdays*, Edward G. Robinson noted that Lancaster was 'showing that animal vitality and suppressed volcano inside that inevitably made him a star.'

'That fine actress Mady Christians, Burt Lancaster and Louisa Horton got under the skin of their parts.'

The Standard

SORRY, WRONG NUMBER

(USA 1948)

RUNNING TIME: 89 minutes

Hal Wallis Production

CAST: Barbara Stanwyck (Leona Stevenson), Burt Lancaster (Henry Stevenson), Ann Richards (Sally Hunt Lord), Wendell Corey (Dr Alexander), Harold Vermilyea (Waldo Evans), Ed Begley (James Cotterell), Leif Erickson (Fred Lord), William Conrad (Morano), John Bromfield (Joe-Detective)

DIRECTOR: Anatole Litvak
PRODUCERS: Hal B. Wallis and Anatole Litvak
SCREENPLAY: Lucille Fletcher from her radio play
PRODUCTION DESIGNERS: Hans Dreier and Earl Hedrick
DIRECTOR OF PHOTOGRAPHY: Sol Polito
EDITOR: Warren Low
MUSIC: Franz Waxman
COSTUMES: Edith Head

PLOT SYNOPSIS:

Leona Stevenson, a spoiled, neurotic, bedridden hypochondriac is alone on the top floor of her Manhattan townhouse one sultry evening. She tries to reach her husband Henry by telephone and in a crossed line connection overhears a conversation between two men who are plotting the murder of a woman later that same evening. She 'phones the police who note her observations with casual indifference.

Her husband, an ambitious younger man, has been attracted by her wealth and their marriage has resulted in his employment in the vast drugs empire owned by Leona's father. However, Henry's ambition has overreached his ability and, alienated by Leona's dominance, Henry is now heavily in debt to a group of gangsters and about to face the consequences. In sheer desperation Henry has hired two men to kill his wife and the resulting insurance money will pay his debts.

Back in the apartment Leona grows increasingly hysterical as, through a series of 'phone calls, she faces the slowly dawning prospect that she had overheard the plotting of her own murder. She frantically attempts to contact her husband for help but, unknown to her, he is awaiting the fateful moment, listening on an extension. The enormity of what is transpiring strikes home but Henry realises that he can only save Leona's life by endangering his own. Now it is too late to save her and the contracted killers move in for their 11.15 pm appointment. When Henry next 'phones home a strange male voice answers; 'Sorry, wrong number.' Leona has met her killers.

COMMENT:

Sorry, Wrong Number continued Lancaster's move away from a plain diet of action rôles. Lucille Fletcher's twenty-two minute radio play had proved a triumph for Agnes Moorehead who gave a *tour de force* performance in the rôle of Leona Stevenson. Fletcher was asked to expand her work into a full-length motion picture and Barbara Stanwyck was cast in the lead rôle.

34

Barbara Stanwyck *(Photo: Hal Wallis Production)*

Lancaster readily accepted the strong supporting rôle of Leona's desperate, scheming husband. He commented; 'I really sweated bullets on that one. This was the first part with which I couldn't identify Lancaster on screen.'

The star duo of Lancaster and Stanwyck repeated their rôles in a one hour Lux Radio Theatre Show during January 1950. Stanwyck was nominated for the Academy Award as Best Actress of 1948 but lost to Jane Wyman as *Johnny Belinda*.

'With Anatole Litvak's brilliant direction, and taut performances by Barbara Stanwyk, Burt Lancaster and the others, the show is calculated to scare the wits out of a spectator . . . Both of the principals succeed in holding *Sorry, Wrong Number* to its mood of savage and unrelenting horror.'

New York Times

KISS THE BLOOD OFF MY HANDS

(UK: BLOOD ON MY HANDS)

(USA 1948)

RUNNING TIME: 80 minutes

Norma Productions

CAST: Joan Fontaine (Jane Wharton), Burt Lancaster (Bill Saunders), Robert Newton (Harry Carter), Lewis L. Russell (Tom Widgery), Aminta Dyne (Landlady), Gryelda Hervey (Mrs Paton), Jay Novello (Sea Captain), Colin Keith-Johnston (Judge), Reginald Sheffield (Superintendent), Campbell Copelin (Publican)

DIRECTOR: Norman Foster
PRODUCER: Richard Vernon
ASSOCIATE PRODUCER: Norman Deming
SCREENPLAY: Leonardo Bercovici from the novel by Gerald Butler
ART DIRECTOR: Bernard Herzbrun
DIRECTOR OF PHOTOGRAPHY: Russell Metty
EDITOR: Milton Carruth
SOUND: Leslie I. Carey and Corson Jowett
MUSIC: Miklos Rosza

PLOT SYNOPSIS:
    London. Canadian merchant sailor Bill Saunders is finding it hard to readjust to the post-war world, his experiences as a prisoner-of-war have left his nerves shattered and his temper unpredictable. In sheer rage he lashes out at a man in a public bar and unintentionally kills him. He flees from the police and escapes by climbing through the window of a nearby boarding house. The room is occupied by a lonely, young nurse, Jane Wharton. Unaware that he is a murderer she takes pity on him and allows him to shelter in her room until the following evening.
    Their chance encounter develops, they see each other regularly and fall in love. Jane manages to find him a job as a van-driver at the clinic where she works. However, the idyll doesn't last; the murder has been witnessed by Carter, a shady Cockney character who has only blackmail on his mind. Carter finds Bill and pressurises him into drug-smuggling; he is to take drugs from the clinic and transport them to the Continent. In return Carter has secured free passage from the country to allow the two lovers a fresh start in life. However, Carter is not satisfied with the deal and starts making advances to Jane. In a fit of hysteria she kills him. The two decide to face the future together and wait for the law to take its course.

COMMENT:
    Lancaster chose the Gerald Butler novel as the first film for his new company, Norma, and hired Joan Fontaine as his co-star.
    Butler's book had sold 232,000 copies in Britain alone but the film version was flawed by choosing fog-shrouded Hollywood sound stages to depict old London

36

(Photo: Norma Productions) Joan Fontaine

town. Lancaster faced several problems on the production side; his pregnant co-star fell ill and had to be allowed time off to recover and inclement weather, including heavy rain, meant that several exterior scenes had to be postponed. The title, more suggestive of a horror film than a gangster melodrama, was also problematic; at various times during the production it was known as *The Unafraid*.

Kiss the Blood off My Hands was only moderately successful and unrepresentative of the later films that Lancaster's company would initiate.

CRISS CROSS

(USA 1949)
RUNNING TIME: 87 minutes

Universal International

CAST: Burt Lancaster (Steve Thompson), Yvonne De Carlo (Anna), Dan Duryea (Slim Dundee), Stephen McNally (Pete Ramirez), Richard Long (Slade Thompson), Tom Pedi (Vincent), Percy Helton (Frank), Alan Napier (Finchley), Griff Barnett (Pop), Edna M. Holland (Mrs Thompson), Tony Curtis (Gigolo)

DIRECTOR: Robert Siodmak
PRODUCER: Michael Kraike
SCREENPLAY: Daniel Fuchs from the novel by Don Tracy
ART DIRECTORS: Bernard Herzbrun and Boris Leven
DIRECTOR OF PHOTOGRAPHY: Franz Planer
EDITOR: Ted J. Kent
SOUND: Leslie I. Carey and Richard De Weese
MUSIC: Miklos Rozsa
COSTUMES: Yvonne Wood

PLOT SYNOPSIS:
Steve Thompson, a muscular but none-too-bright young man, returns to his former home in Los Angeles and to his old job as a guard on a money-carrying armoured car. He finds himself still besotted with his ex-wife Anna despite the fact that she is now remarried to a smooth operating criminal, Slim Dundee.

In order to be nearer Anna, Steve agrees to take part in a large scale robbery masterminded by Slim and involving a raid on Steve's armoured car. The sadistic Slim double-crosses him, absconding with the proceeds and badly wounding Steve. When Slim's gang realise that Slim has attempted to double-cross everyone they kidnap Steve from hospital. He pays them to lead him to Anna who, concerned only for herself, is preparing to flee with his share of the money. Still badly injured he is deserted by the heartless Anna. However, she quickly returns, preferring his caring company to the prospect of a vengeful Slim, gun in hand. The two are happily reunited, much to Steve's pleasure, but Slim fires two shots, killing both Steve and Anna. In the background can be heard the noise of police sirens; Slim faces imminent capture.

COMMENT:
Lancaster committed himself to *Criss Cross*, a further gangster yarn, when it was in the planning stages as the next Mark Hellinger production. However, Hellinger died of a heart attack at the tragically early age of forty-four whilst completing work on his previous feature *The Naked City*.

Criss Cross is interesting now for introducing the young Tony Curtis to the screen and as an example of the routine, popular entertainments provided by Hollywood in its heyday and now more likely to fill an episode of a weekly series.

(Photo: Universal International Pictures) Yvonne De Carlo

'A film unedifying and not original in plot, but one which is expert in the use of its own idiom, and which is directed with touches of imagination.'

The Times

'Most of it consists of an account by Burt Lancaster of how he foolishly became a robber . . . As Mr Lancaster is no great shakes either as a raconteur or as a thinker the result is a pretty dull monologue in words of one syllable.'

Daily Mail

ROPE OF SAND

(USA 1949)

RUNNING TIME: 105 minutes

Hal Wallis Production

CAST: Burt Lancaster (Mike Davis), Paul Henreid (Vogel), Claude Rains (Martingale), Corinne Calvet (Suzanne), Peter Lorre (Toady), John Bromfield (Thompson), Sam Jaffe (Dr Hunter), Mike Mazurki (Pierson), Kenny Washington (John), Edmond Breen (Chairman), Hayden Rorke (Ingram)

DIRECTOR: William Dieterle
PRODUCER: Hal Wallis
SCREENPLAY: Walter Doniger
DIRECTOR OF PHOTOGRAPHY: Charles Lang
MUSIC: Franz Waxman

PLOT SYNOPSIS:

Mike Davis, a tough hunting guide, returns to the South African diamond-mining town of Diamantesberg. His one intention is to find a cache of diamonds hidden in the Prohibited Area. He has secretly discovered the cache whilst on a rescue mission. Davis is not the only one interested in the diamonds, they are equally coveted by two villainous mine operators, the ruthless, charming Martingale and the equally charming but less refined Vogel who is in charge of the Diamond Area.

Vogel is restrained from using torture on Mike by Martingale who has a more subtle means of persuasion in mind. He has hired the pretty Suzanne to extract the necessary information from Mike. The two fall in love although Mike remains dubious of her motives. Warned of the dangers involved Mike nonetheless enters the Prohibited Area and is captured by Vogel. Suzanne frees him and, eventually, discovering the diamonds, the duo head for freedom leaving Vogel stranded in the desert.

Vogel returns to town and, enraged by his failure, kills a local doctor. Suzanne is accused of the murder and Mike offers the diamonds to secure her safety. Still scheming, Martingale forces Vogel to sign a confession and engineers a fight between Mike and Vogel in which the latter is killed. Mike is cleared of any charges and, together with Suzanne, sails for America.

COMMENT:

Rope of Sand put no great strain on Lancaster the actor but provided enjoyable escapist entertainment. Claude Rains, Paul Henreid and Peter Lorre, reunited from *Casablanca*, had seen better films but the generally strong cast helped maintain a degree of credibility in the colourful proceedings.

The scenes of the diamond area in Diamantesberg were filmed at Yuma in Arizona. In America the rather sadistic behaviour attributed to the principal villains caused problems with the censors.

(Photo: Hal Wallis Production) Peter Lorre

'It has a fight or a whipping every quarter of an hour or so and seems otherwise to have no point at all . . . a film dedicated to brutality.'

The Guardian

'The film is atavistic, a throw-back to the days of the silent film when the screen had no need to strive after the subtleties of sophistication. It is a very violent, very silly and at moments not unentertaining.'

The Times

THE FLAME AND THE ARROW

(USA 1950)
RUNNING TIME: 89 minutes

Norma Productions

CAST: Burt Lancaster (Dardo), Virginia Mayo (Anne), Robert Douglas (Alessandro), Aline Macmahon (Nonna Bartoli), Frank Allenby (Ulrich), Nick Cravat (Piccolo), Lynne Baggett (Francesca), Gordon Gerbert (Rudi)

DIRECTOR: Jacques Tourneur
PRODUCER: Harold Hecht and Frank Ross
SCREENPLAY: Waldo Salt
ART DIRECTOR: Edward Carrere
DIRECTOR OF PHOTOGRAPHY: Ernest Haller
EDITOR: Alan Crossland
MUSIC: Max Steiner

PLOT SYNOPSIS:
Lombardy, Italy. Dardo the Arrow, a swashbuckling, acrobatic mountaineer stands for liberty and freedom from oppression. He is a hero to the local people and much loved by his wily band of men. He plans to lead the people in a revolt against the Hessian invaders of his country. When the Hessian leader, Ulrich, recruits a band of German mercenaries to strengthen his hold on the country Dardo decides it is time to act.

Dardo's son is held captive in Ulrich's castle and to gain a bargaining wedge Dardo and his men capture Ulrich's beautiful niece Anne. Anne falls for the handsome rebel and realises that his cause is just. Meanwhile Ulrich proclaims that five of the local citizenry will be killed unless Dardo surrenders. Dardo complies but has secretly plotted with the hanging party to wear a harness which saves his neck and leaves Ulrich with the impression that he has perished.

To celebrate their triumph the Hessians stage a large celebration in the castle and hire a troop of entertainers – jugglers, tumblers and acrobats. The entertainers are, of course, Dardo and his men in disguise. They proceed to free Dardo's son and kill the despised Ulrich. With success all round Dardo sweeps the princess Anne into his arms for a happy ending.

COMMENT:
The Flame and the Arrow was a project close to the heart of Lancaster, a swashbuckler of panache and graceful agility. Before filming, 'Lang and Cravat' limbered up by reviving their old act for two weeks at the Cole Brothers Circus on a salary of eleven thousand dollars per week. Filmed at Warner Brothers the impression of following in the footsteps of Errol Flynn can only have been encouraged by the use of sets still standing from *The Adventures of Don Juan* and *The Adventures of Robin Hood*, two Flynn successes.

As a publicity stunt Warner Brothers offered a million dollars to anyone who could prove that Lancaster did not do his own stunts in the film. By a legal technicality it would have been impossible for anyone to claim. However, apart from three sequences everything on screen was Lancaster's own work.

(Photo: Norma Productions)

The Flame and the Arrow wound up on the American chart of money-making films in 1950 at position eleven, with takings of almost three million dollars.

'Burt Lancaster's acrobatics, in the Fairbank's tradition, are energetic, and the production as a whole, excellent.'

Monthly Film Bulletin

'Whether swinging from chandeliers, scampering across rooftops, leaping to and from balconies or demonstrating his ability with a bow and arrow, Lancaster rose spectacularly to the occasion.'

The Warner Brothers Story

MISTER 880

(USA 1950)

RUNNING TIME: 90 minutes

20th Century Fox

CAST: Burt Lancaster (Steve Buchanan), Dorothy McGuire (Ann Winslow), Edmund Gwenn ('Skipper' Miller), Millard Mitchell (Mac), Minor Watson (Judge), Howard St John (Secret Service Chief), Hugh Sanders (Thad Mitchell), James Millican (Olie)

DIRECTOR: Edmund Golding
PRODUCER: Julian Blaustein
SCREENPLAY: Robert Riskin
ART DIRECTORS: Lyle Wheeler and George W. Davis
DIRECTOR OF PHOTOGRAPHY: Joseph La Shelle
EDITOR: Robert Fritch
SOUND: Arthur L. Kirbach and Roger Heman
MUSIC: Sol Kaplan
COSTUMES: Travilla

PLOT SYNOPSIS:

For over ten years the Treasury Department has been baffled by a mysterious criminal, an expert counterfeiter known as Mister 880. Government agent Steve Buchanan is assigned to the case and begins his investigation. He traces one of the forged bills to a girl, Ann, and, although this lead proves unprofitable, Steve is convinced that Mister 880 remains somewhere in the neighbourhood.

Mister 880 is, in fact, 'Skipper' Miller, an amiable old gentleman whose nominal profession is that of a junk dealer. For ten years he had been printing between forty and fifty single dollar bills every month. He had only printed enough to live on as he didn't want to be a burden on the taxpayer. He has escaped detection by printing such a small number of bills and spreading them over a wide area. Eventually his activities are uncovered by Steve and he is discovered to be lodging at the same house as Ann.

Miller is subsequently brought to trial. However, with Steve's sympathetic account of his virtually harmless activities and Miller's own quaint logic, the judge is inclined towards leniency. Miller is sentenced to four months imprisonment and a fine of one dollar.

COMMENT:

Mister 880, an amiable lighthearted comedy, provided a diverting change of pace for Lancaster although Edmund Gwenn had the best rôle as the genial counterfeiter.

The film was based on a true story which was first featured in an article in *The New Yorker* magazine by St Clair McKelway. The real counterfeiter, Case Number 880, had printed only crude one dollar bills, never passed them to the same person twice and did escape detection for a decade. Treasury efforts had included visits to ten thousand shopkeepers, radio broadcasts and over two hundred thousand handbills were distributed on how to recognise a phoney note.

(Photo: 20th Century Fox) Dorothy McGuire and Edmund Gwenn

Scriptwriter Robert Riskin had been a frequent collaborator of Frank Capra's and their traditional elements of sentimentality and whimsy are pleasantly to the fore here.

'A neat, deft, beautifully acted comedy about a gentle smalltime counterfeiter.'
Sunday Pictorial

'Burt Lancaster as the detective and Dorothy McGuire as the inevitable girlfriend, are as pleasant to watch as they obviously are nice to know.'
Sunday Dispatch

'Dorothy McGuire and Burt Lancaster are excellent.'
News of the World

VENGEANCE VALLEY

(USA 1951)
RUNNING TIME: 82 minutes

Metro-Goldwyn-Mayer

CAST: Burt Lancaster (Owen Daybright), Robert Walker (Lee Strobie), Joanne Dru (Jen Strobie), Sally Forrest (Lily), John Ireland (Hub Fasken), Ray Collins (Arch Strobie), Carleton Carpenter (Hewie), Ted de Corsica (Herb Backett), Hugh O'Brian (Dick Fasken), Will Wright (Mr Willoughby)

DIRECTOR: Richard Thorpe
PRODUCER: Nicholas Nayfack
SCREENPLAY: Irving Ravetch from the novel by Luke Short
ART DIRECTORS: Cedric Gibbons and Malcolm Brown
DIRECTOR OF PHOTOGRAPHY: George Folsey
EDITOR: Conrad A. Nervig
MUSIC: Rudolph G. Kopp

PLOT SYNOPSIS:
Aging patriarch Arch Strobie has two sons, Lee Strobie and Owen Daybright, the latter adopted. The two men couldn't be more different if they tried – Lee; callous, avaricious and indifferent to the consequences of his actions. Owen; steadfast, responsible and hardworking. During the Spring cattle roundup on the ranch family rivalries are resolved.

Lee has abandoned his wife Jen, and his association with a local girl, Lily, has resulted in her pregnancy. Owen attempts to keep the news of Lee's misdemeanours from his father and is hotly pursued by the girl's vengeful brothers who assume that he is responsible for her condition. Meanwhile, Lee has persuaded his father to give him a share of the ranch, whilst plotting to make off with all the cattle and pin the blame on Owen. Owen attempts to stop him and a showdown between the two brothers seems inevitable. In a gunfight, the nasty younger brother is killed. Owen returns to Lee's widow Jen whom he has always secretly loved.

COMMENT:
Lancaster's first Western was distinctly out of the rut, eschewing the traditional 'cowboys and Indians' formula, settling instead for soap opera on the range. The original story appeared as a serial in the *Saturday Evening Post* and later as a novel. Robert Walker, cast against type, as the amoral brother seemed to enjoy his villainy in one of his last completed films. The self-censorship practised by the Hollywood film-makers of the period, under the dictates of the Production Code, ensured that Walker met his comeuppance.

'The movie gives the customers plenty of violence; hero Lancaster's brawls net him a badly mauled head, a knife gash in the side, a bullet in the arm.'
Time

(Photo: Metro-Goldwyn-Mayer)

JIM THORPE – ALL-AMERICAN

(UK: MAN OF BRONZE)

(USA 1951)
RUNNING TIME: 105 minutes

Warner Brothers

CAST: Burt Lancaster (Jim Thorpe), Charles Bickford ('Pop' Warner), Steve Cochran (Peter Allendine), Phyllis Thaxter (Margaret Miller), Dick Wesson (Ed Guyac), Jack Big Head (Little Boy), Suni Warcloud (Wally Denny), Al Mejia (Louis Tewanema), Hubie Kerns (Ashenbrunner)

DIRECTOR: Michael Curtiz
PRODUCER: Everett Freeman
SCREENPLAY: Douglas Morrow and Everett Freeman
ART DIRECTOR: Edward Carrere
DIRECTOR OF PHOTOGRAPHY: Ernest Haller
EDITOR: Folmar Blangsted
MUSIC: Max Steiner

PLOT SYNOPSIS:

Jim Thorpe, a young Red Indian from Oklahoma, is encouraged by his father to leave their reservation and find his way in the world by gaining a good education. In 1907 he enrolls at the Carlisle Indian School in Pennsylvania and, although undistinguished academically, he is outstanding on the sports field. Encouraged by the school's coach, Pop Warner, he becomes an all-events champion and All-American footballer. Thorpe seeks employment as a sports coach and wants to settle down and marry. He is not employed on racial grounds.

In 1912 he enter the fifth Olympic Games in Stockholm, winning the pentathlon and decathlon events and setting new records. However, it is discovered that he has played professional baseball which infringes his amateur status and he is disqualified, stripped of his medals and the records. He becomes a professional baseball player and then a footballer but is further dogged by tragedy when his son dies. His misfortunes continue when he turns to drink and his wife can no longer cope with his sullen moods and fits of depression. She leaves him.

In 1932 Thorpe visits the Olympics in Los Angeles and is reminded of his past accomplishments. He makes a decision to start afresh and try to pull his life together. He manages to find work as a truck driver and begins to coach youngsters in his spare time.

COMMENT:

Before making *The Flame and the Arrow* Lancaster signed a contract with Warner Brothers allowing him to co-produce pictures with the studio, in return Warner Brothers could employ him as an actor in their own productions. The company had owned the rights to Jim Thorpe's story for many years and now held an option on an ideal candidate for the part.

(Photo: Warner Bros.)

Lancaster was attracted to the athletic elements in the story but also found the issue of racial prejudice appealed to his social conscience. Thorpe had spent some time in Hollywood as an extra and was employed on the film as a technical adviser.

'Burt Lancaster seems particularly well suited to play a character consisting almost exclusively of brawn and persecution complex, and is thoroughly convincing in the athletic sequences.'

Daily Mail

TEN TALL MEN

(USA 1951)

RUNNING TIME: 97 minutes

Norma Productions for Columbia

CAST: Burt Lancaster (Sgt. Mike Kincaid), Gilbert Roland (Cpl. Luid Delgado), Kieron Moore (Cpl. Pierre Molier), George Tobias (Londos), Jody Lawrence (Mahla), Gerald Mohr (Hussin), John Dehner (Jardine), Nick Dennis (Mouse), Mike Mazurki (Roshko), Gerald Mohr (Caid Hussin), Ian Macdonald (Lustig)

DIRECTOR: Willis Goldbeck
PRODUCER: Harold Hecht
SCREENPLAY: Roland Kibbee and Frank Davis from a story by James Warner Bellah and Willis Goldbeck
ART DIRECTOR: Carl Anderson
DIRECTOR OF PHOTOGRAPHY: William Snyder
EDITOR: William Lyon
SOUND: George Cooper
MUSIC: David Buttolph
COSTUMES: Jean Louis

PLOT SYNOPSIS:
Sergeant Mike Kincaid, aided by Corporals Luid Delgado and Pierre Molier and seven other men, forms a rough, tough special unit within the French Foreign Legion. The squad accept a dangerous mission – to harrass and wear down the amassed forces of the Riffs and thwart their expected attack on the city in which the main body of the Legion is garrisoned.

Led by Mike they work on an adventurous plan. The squad kidnap Mahla, a Riff princess and daughter of the chieftain. Her forthcoming marriage to Hussin would have cemented relations between the normally fractious tribes and united them in their opposition to the Legion. The tribes' schemes have even included taking over the country.

Hussin retaliates and the squad need all their wits to survive the attacks by Hussin's men, made even more treacherous by the cover given them in a sandstorm. The Legion and Hussin's forces join battle, Kincaid and his men triumph and Hussin is killed.

COMMENT:
Lancaster sought none of the significance of *Jim Thorpe – All-American* in *Ten Tall Men*, a larkish, far-fetched adventure yarn purely intent on entertaining its large audience.

Early in the history of Hecht-Lancaster productions Lancaster deployed his sharp awareness of commercial fare to the company's financial gain – *Ten Tall Men* was one such lucrative outing. Such a policy helped balance the less successful ventures like their first non-Lancaster film, *The First Time*, a mild domestic comedy made in 1952, or the socially committed *Take a Giant Step*, a 1959 drama about the difficulties encountered by American blacks.

(Photo: *Norma Productions*)

'*Ten Tall Men*, a tall adventure tale of the French Foreign Legion, treats its old formula so lightly that it becomes the 'beau jest' of the genre. All that is missing is the sight of Bob Hope and Bing Crosby.'

Time

THE CRIMSON PIRATE

(United Kingdom 1952)
RUNNING TIME: 104 minutes

Norma Productions for Warner Brothers

CAST: Burt Lancaster (Captain Vallo), Nick Cravat (Ojo), Eva Bartok (Consuelo), Leslie Bradley (Baron Gruda), Torin Thatcher (Humble Bellows), Margot Grahame (Bianca), James Hayter (Prudence), Noel Purcell (Pablo Murphy), Frederick Leister (Sebastian El-Libre), Christopher Lee (Attaché)

DIRECTOR: Robert Siodmak
PRODUCER: Harold Hecht
SCREENPLAY: Roland Kibbee
ART DIRECTOR: Paul Sheriff
DIRECTOR OF PHOTOGRAPHY: Otto Heller
EDITOR: Jack Harris
SOUND: A.E. Rudolph
PRODUCTION MANAGER: Terry Hunter
MUSIC: William Alwyn
COSTUMES: Margaret Furse

PLOT SYNOPSIS:
Somewhere in the Caribbean, the late eighteenth century: Captain Vallo and his crew sail the seven seas. Posing as a death ship, the Crimson Pirate successfully attacks and boards a ship of the King's navy. The prize is an armoury of weapons and the King's envoy Baron Gruda. Vallo plans to sell the arms to El Libre, the rebel leader on the island of Cobra, for 50,000 gold florins, then sell El Libre and his men to Baron Gruda for a further 100,000 gold florins.

Sailing under the King's colours Vallo drops anchor at Cobra and goes ashore with his lieutenant, Ojo, to seek out El Libre. The rebel leader is imprisoned but his attractive daughter Consuelo persuades Vallo to free her father. Impersonating Baron Gruda, Vallo is given El Libre and Professor Prudence into his custody, managing to flee when his deception is uncovered.

Caught between his romance with Consuelo and the plundering pirate code of his men Vallo is forced to let El Libre escape with the arms under the cloak of night, unbeknownst to the crew.

The real Baron Gruda arrives and conspires with the mutineers on the *Crimson Pirate* to oust Vallo as Captain, installing Humble Bellows in his place. Gruda kills El Libre, captures Consuelo, sets Vallo adrift with Ojo and Professor Prudence and then drugs the crew, assuming total control. The trio at sea however have escaped and manage to reach shore.

To save the lives of the islanders Consuelo agrees to marry the Governer and rule in the King's name. Dressed as women Vallo, Ojo and the Professor infiltrate the wedding ceremony. With the appliance of science, including a hot-air balloon, nitroglycerin and a prototype submarine, the trio rescue Consuelo, kill the Baron and free the islanders from tyranny.

Nick Cravat *(Photo: Norma Productions*

COMMENT:

The Crimson Pirate allegedly began life as a fairly straight-laced pirate adventure but, during production, Lancaster and company decided to play for laughs and make a spoof of the genre.

Continuing his association with Warner Brothers Lancaster cut costs by filming *The Crimson Pirate* from their British base at Teddington Studios by the Thames. The cast spent four months filming on the island of Ischia, an Italian fishing community in the Bay of Naples near Capri. The Mediterranean acted as a stand-in for the Caribbean and two ships were specially constructed at Villefranche in the French Mediterranean. Filming was completed in November 1951 and, in Britain, the picture was released for the Christmas holidays in 1952. Interviewed in Britain Lancaster said; 'This one is lusty and gusty. We're throwing everything in. It has taken five years off my life already.'

'Mr Lancaster is the best swashbuckler in the business.'

Daily Worker

'an enjoyable nonsensical piece of cutlassery in Technicolour, splendid and improbable acrobatics from Burt Lancaster and Nick Cravat, just the ticket for bloodthirsty schoolboys.'

The Sunday Times

COME BACK LITTLE SHEBA

(USA 1952)

RUNNING TIME: 96 minutes

Hal Wallis Production for Paramount

CAST: Burt Lancaster (Doc Delaney), Shirley Booth (Lola Delaney), Terry Moore (Marie Buckholder), Richard Jaekel (Turk Fisher), Philip Ober (Ed Anderson), Edwin Max (Elmo Huston), Lisa Golm (Mrs Coffman), Walter Kelley (Brice), Paul McVey (Postman)

DIRECTOR: Daniel Mann
PRODUCER: Hal Wallis
SCREENPLAY: Ketti Frings from the play by William Inge
ART DIRECTORS: Hal Pereira and Henry Bumstead
DIRECTOR OF PHOTOGRAPHY: James Wong Howe
EDITOR: Warren Low
MUSIC: Franz Waxman
COSTUMES: Edith Head

PLOT SYNOPSIS:

In a small town Doc and Lola Delaney, a lonely, middle-aged couple, live out a marriage long dead. Doc had married Lola only from a sense of obligation – she was pregnant. They married, the child died and Lola was unable to have any more children. This unhappiness has corroded their union; Doc was unable to finish his course at medical school, never qualifying as a doctor and seeking a living as a chiropracter. Frustrated by his ill-fortune he has turned to drink and is a member of Alcoholics Anonymous. It is now a year since he has taken a drink. Lola has drifted with Doc into a hollow existence, pampering and spoiling her dog, Little Sheba, who has gone missing.

When Marie, an attractive student, rents a room from the Delaneys their uneasy life in disturbed. Lola mourns her lost youth and Doc find Marie embodying the beauty and hope that his life has lacked for so long. However, Marie is less than perfect, although engaged she is involved in a passionate affair with Turk, a college athlete. When Doc learns of their liaison he is bitterly disillusioned and hits the bottle. In a drunken rage he turns on Lola, whom he holds responsible for his many disappointments, and attacks her with a knife. Doc is taken to hospital for treatment. On his return there is a tentative reconciliation with Lola, each realising that they have only the other in life.

COMMENT:

On Broadway middle-aged Shirley Booth had won five major awards for her work in William Inge's *Come Back Little Sheba*. When Hal Wallis bought the screen rights it was considered too risky to entrust the film version to Booth who had never appeared before the cameras. Wallis attempted to cast Bette Davis and Sidney Blackmer in the main rôles. Davis rejected the move although she later admitted that it was one of the biggest mistakes she ever made. Wallis decided to cast Booth and was finally convinced by Lancaster that he should accept him as Doc; it made sound commercial sense as well.

(Photo: Hal Wallis Production)

Filming on locations near the University of Southern California the production enjoyed the luxury of a week's rehearsals prior to shooting. Booth won the Academy Award as Best Actress and, on the strength of that, the film was the number thirteen money-maker in the 1953 American charts, earning three and a half million dollars.

'the excellence of Mr Lancaster as the frustrated, inarticulate spouse, weak-willed and sweetly passive, should not be overlooked.'

New York Times

'Burt Lancaster, looking distinguished with his hair cut and parted, shows a new and unexpected talent as the husband.'

Daily Telegraph

'Mr Lancaster suggests with extraordinary skill the agonised division of the doctor's mind.'

The Times

TO1S180

SOUTH SEA WOMAN

(USA 1953)
RUNNING TIME: 89 minutes

Warner Brothers

CAST: Burt Lancaster (Sgt. O'Hearn), Virginia Mayo (Ginger Martin), Chuck Connors (David White), Arthur Shields (Donovan USNR), Barry Kelley (Col. Hickman), Leon Askin (Marchand), Veola Vonn (Mme Duval), Robert Sweeney (Lt. Miller), Hayden Rorke (Lt. Fears), Raymond Greenleaf (Rear-Admiral Peabody)

DIRECTOR: Arthur Lubin
PRODUCER: Sam Bischoff
SCREENPLAY: Edwin Blum from the play by William M. Rankin
ART DIRECTOR: Edward Carrere
DIRECTOR OF PHOTOGRAPHY: Ted McCord
EDITOR: Clarence Kolster
SOUND: Francis J. Scheid
MUSIC: David Buttolph
COSTUMES: Moss Malory

PLOT SYNOPSIS:

Jim O'Hearn, a hell-raising marine sergeant is on trial, charged with desertion, stealing a yacht and sinking a nightclub. Against O'Hearn's wishes Ginger Martin, a nightclub camera girl, appears as a witness and, through her testimony, the court learns the truth behind the accusations.

The catalogue of events she recounts begins two weeks before Pearl Harbour when the American marines were ordered out of Shanghai. O'Hearn's best friend, Davey White, has gone absent from camp to marry Ginger but, when her employer refuses to allow her to leave, a brawl develops. O'Hearn has followed Davey and he is inveigled into the fight. The trio escape in a motor boat which is unfortunately tied to the foundations; hence the sinking of the nightclub. On an island hideaway there is a conflict of interests – O'Hearn is itching to join in the combat while Davey is more preoccupied with his interest in Ginger. The three set sail again, stealing a German yacht and freeing the French prisoners on board. They engage a Japanese destroyer and, in the resulting fray, Davey is killed whilst despatching some TNT down the smokestack. Victorious, O'Hearn and Ginger are later rescued by the American Navy.

The judgement at the trial clears O'Hearn of all charges and posthumously awards the Congressional Medal of Honour to Davey. O'Hearn and Ginger decide to marry.

COMMENT:

After the acclaim for his newly discovered acting ability in *Come Back Little Sheba*, *South Sea Woman* sticks out like the proverbial sore thumb. It is the weakest, most fancifully plotted film that he ever appeared in during his 'he-man' days. However, there is a logical explanation. Under the terms of his contract with

Virginia Mayo *(Photo: Warner Bros.)*

Warner Brothers he owed them a film and *South Sea Woman* was the script they chose when asking him to honour that commitment.

He fulfilled his obligations later the same year by making a brief guest appearance in the Jane Powell-Gordon MacRae musical *Three Sailors and a Girl*.

'That Burt Lancaster is required to run around the island in a grass skirt and frolic with the proprietress of the local bawdy house is characteristic of the bad taste of the whole film, which can only be described as a disagreeable mistake.'
Monthly Film Bulletin

FROM HERE TO ETERNITY

(USA 1953)
RUNNING TIME: 118 minutes

Columbia Pictures

CAST: Burt Lancaster (Sgt. Warden), Montgomery Clift (Pte. Prewitt), Frank
Sinatra (Pte. Angelo Maggio), Deborah Kerr (Karen Holmes), Donna Reed
(Lorene), Ernest Borgnine (Sgt. Judson), Philip Ober (Capt. Holmes), Jack
Warden (Cpl. Buckley), Mickey Shaughnessy (Sgt. Leva)

DIRECTOR: Fred Zinneman
PRODUCER: Buddy Adler
SCRRENPLAY: Dalton Trumbo from the novel by James Jones
ART DIRECTOR: Gary Odell
DIRECTOR OF PHOTOGRAPHY: Burnett Guffey
EDITOR: William Lyon
SOUND: Lodge Cunningham
MUSIC: George Duning
COSTUMES: Jean Louis

PLOT SYNOPSIS:
The Summer of 1941. Private Robert E. Lee Prewitt, an outstanding bugler and
accomplished middleweight boxer, is assigned to Schofield Barracks in Honolulu.
The company commander is Captain Dana Holmes but the real strength of the
company stems from the organisational abilities of Sergeant Warden, a tough,
fair-minded man with a contempt for the officer class.

Holmes expects Prewitt to box for the company but he stubbornly refuses; in
one encounter he has blinded his opponent and vowed never to fight again.
Holmes applies pressure and other members of the company cold-shoulder him.
His only friend is the wiry, hot-headed private Angelo Maggio.

Over the summer, Warden falls in love with Holmes' bored wife Karen and
their passionate affair develops into a lasting relationship. Prewitt meets Lorene,
an attractive money-grabbing prostitute who is fascinated by him and a genuine
friendship grows.

Maggio's reckless actions land him in the stockade where he is badly treated by
the sadistic Sergeant 'Fatso' Judson. Fatally wounded, he escapes, dying in the
arms of his friend Prewitt. Prewitt retaliates by slaying Fatso in a knife duel but is
himself critically wounded. Going AWOL he stays with Lorene to recover.

On 7 December 1941 there is a surprise attack by the Japanese on Pearl
Harbour. Prewitt is determined to return to his company but is accidentally killed
by his own men. Warden puts all thoughts of his romantic involvement with Karen
aside to apply himself to the thing he knows best — soldiering. Karen and Lorene
return to America on the same ship.

Deborah Kerr *(Photo: Columbia Pictures)*

COMMENT:
Now rightly regarded as one of the screen classics, *From Here to Eternity* might have been quite a different film had all the original casting intentions transpired. Columbia studio chief Harry Cohn had spent eighty-two thousand dollars for the screen rights to James Jones hefty novel. Columbia pencilled in either of two of their contract players for the rôle of Prewitt – Aldo Ray or John Derek. Director Zinneman held out for Clift. Eli Wallach was the first choice for the part of Maggio – Sinatra had to beg and borrow favours to be entrusted with the rôle, and it was only a disagreement over the wardrobe which saw Deborah Kerr replace Joan Crawford.

Wallis exacted a stiff price for Lancaster but he won the New York Critics Award and his first Academy Award nomination, losing to William Holden for *Stalag 17*. The film won eight Academy Awards, including Best Picture, the most for a single picture since *Gone with the Wind* and was the second top American money-maker in 1953 with an impressive haul of twelve and a half million dollars.

'Burt Lancaster is a tower of strength, literally and figuratively, as the sergeant, the infinite professional soldier.'

Daily Mail

'The three male leads in the film turn in the finest performances of their careers.'
Time

HIS MAJESTY O'KEEFE

(United Kingdom 1953)
RUNNING TIME: 90 minutes

Norma Productions

CAST: Burt Lancaster (Captain O'Keefe), Joan Rice (Dalabo), Andre Morell (Alfred Tetens), Abraham Sofaer (Fatumak), Archie Savage (Boogulroo), Benson Fong (Mr Chou), Tessa Prendergast (Kakofel), Lloyd Berrell (Inifel), Charles Horvath (Bully Hayes), Philip Ahn (Sien Tang), Guy Doleman (Weber), Grant Taylor (Lt. Brenner)

DIRECTOR: Byron Haskin
PRODUCER: Harold Hecht
SCREENPLAY: Borden Chase and James Hill
ART DIRECTORS: Edward S. Haworth and W. Simpson Robinson
DIRECTOR OF PHOTOGRAPHY: Otto Heller
EDITOR: Manuel del Campo
SOUND: Harold King
PRODUCTION MANAGER: Stanley Haynes
MUSIC: Robert Farnon
COSTUMES: Marjorie Best and Liz Hemmings

PLOT SYNOPSIS:
Opportunist South Seas Yankee adventurer Captain O'Keefe is thrown overboard by his mutinous crew and swims ashore on the Island of Yap. He quickly realises there is a fortune to be made from the copra resources on the island if he can persuade the natives to work for him. Tetens, a failed German trader, explains to him that he can gain the trust of the natives with the one thing that they hold precious – *fei*; huge stones quarried from a far-off island.

O'Keefe arranges his expedition and sets off in search of the *fei* which he discovers along with Dalabo, a beautiful half-caste Polynesian girl. O'Keefe trades with the medicine man of Yap, Fatumak, and they exchange the *fei* for a shipload of copra which O'Keefe transports to Hong Kong. It is there that he marries Dalabo and sets sail for a further lucrative voyage.

However, on his return, O'Keefe finds this island is run by the pirate Bully Hayes, a black-hearted slaver. O'Keefe has grown to love the area and the people so he helps them to reconquer the island, killing Hayes.

As a mark of their respect and gratitude the islanders ask O'Keefe to become their King and he willingly accepts.

COMMENT:
A bread and butter picture after the heights of *From Here to Eternity*, the swashbuckling *His Majesty O'Keefe* was based on true incidents in the eventful life of an Irish adventurer called O'Keefe. The Technicolour production was filmed largely on the Fijian island of Viti Lemu.

His Majesty O'Keefe marked the end of his working relationship with Warner Brothers. From 1954 onwards Hecht-Lancaster worked as a solo company, arranging for the distribution of their films through United Artists.

(Photo: Norma Productions)

'Burt Lancaster rules the roost with well-sustained, self-reliant grin, leaping and fighting among a plethora of native dancers . . .'

Evening News

APACHE

(USA 1954)

RUNNING TIME: 87 minutes

Linden Productions for Hecht-Lancaster Productions

CAST: Burt Lancaster (Massai), Jean Peters (Nalinle), John McIntire (Al Sieber), Charles Buchinsky (Hondo), John Dehner (Weddle), Paul Guilfoyle (Santos), Ian MacDonald (Clagg), Walter Sande (Lt-Col Beck), Morris Ankrum (Dawson), Monte Blue (Geronimo)

DIRECTOR: Robert Aldrich
PRODUCER: Harold Hecht
SCREENPLAY: James E. Webb from the novel *Bronco Apache* by Paul I. Wellman
PRODUCTION DESIGNER: Nicolai Remisoff
DIRECTOR OF PHOTOGRAPHY: Ernest Laszlo
EDITOR: Alan Crosland Jr.
SOUND: Jack Solomon
PRODUCTION MANAGER: Jack R. Berne
MUSIC: David Raksin
COSTUMES: Norma

PLOT SYNOPSIS:

Geronimo has surrendered and the great days of the Apache nation are considered to be over. One resolute warrior, Massai, refuses to give in to the white man and attempts to disrupt the peace negotiations at which Geronimo is to surrender. Massai is captured and sentenced with other members of the Apache tribe to be shipped to reservations in Florida. He escapes *en route* and begins a long, tiring trek back to the lands of the Apache. There he is reunited with his squaw, Nalinle, but her father, Santos, betrays him to the white man and again he is captured and shipped to Florida.

Again Massai escapes and proclaims open season on the white man as well as seeking vengeance for Santos's actions. He believes Nalinle has aided her father in his capture and so he kidnaps her and rides off into the mountains. At first there is only bitterness and distrust between them but soon Massai relents and their love is stronger than ever. They marry according to the tribal rite and spend the winter together in the mountains. By spring Nalinle is pregnant with their first child. Throughout the winter inclement weather has prevented the cavalry patrols from trailing Massai and his bride but, with the spring thaw, the troops begin to move in. As the troops approach Massai prepares for the final showdown. As both sides prepare to fire the first shots, the cry of a new-born child is heard. Massai turns back towards his hut and the soldiers allow him to go on his way unharmed.

COMMENT:

Along with *Broken Arrow*, *Apache* represents the beginning of Hollywood's reappraisal of its approach to the representation of the Red Indian on screen. Dealing with a subdued race the material appealed strongly to Lancaster.

Charles Buchinsky (Bronson) *(Photo: Linden Productions)*

A dispute arose over the ending of the film which was shot efficiently over thirty-four days by director Aldrich. The conclusion of the original script saw Massai senselessly shot in the back. The distributors insisted however that Lancaster's fans would not go to see a film in which their hero died. Initially, Lancaster stood firmly with the director in resisting any changes but eventually compromised, giving in to box-office pressures.

'Burt Lancaster does his strong, stubborn persecuted man stuff in great style.'
Daily Mirror

VERA CRUZ

(USA 1954)

RUNNING TIME: 92 minutes

Flora Productions for Hecht-Lancaster Productions

CAST: Gary Cooper (Benjamin Trane), Burt Lancaster (Joe Erin), Denise Darcel (Countess Marie Duvarre), Cesar Romero (Marquis de Labordère), Sarita Montiel (Nina), George MacReady (Emperor Maximilian), Ernest Borgnine (Donegan), Morris Ankrum (General Aguilar), James McCallion (Little Bit), Jack Lambert (Charlie)

DIRECTOR: Robert Aldrich
PRODUCER: James Hill
SCREENPLAY: Roland Kibbee, James R. Webb and Borden Chase
PRODUCTION DESIGNER: Alfred Ybarra
DIRECTOR OF PHOTOGRAPHY: Ernest Laszlo
EDITOR: Alan Crosland Jr.
SOUND: Manuel Topete, Galina Samperio
PRODUCTION MANAGER: Nate Edwards
MUSIC: Hugo Friedhofer
COSTUMES: Norma

PLOT SYNOPSIS:
Mexico, 1866. Among the many adventurers and opportunists flocking to Mexico during the reign of Emperor Maximilian are Benjamin Trane and Joe Erin. The two decide to join forces and fight for whichever side will pay them the most. Their services are sought by Nina, a voluptuous pickpocket attracted to Trane, who urges them to fight for the rebels, and by the Marquis de Labordère, an aide to Maximilian, who asks them to join the Emperor.

At the ball in the sumptuous Chapultepec the duo meet Countess Marie Duvarre and agree to provide the escort for her journey from Mexico City to Vera Cruz. The territory is full of hazards none more perilous than the marauding supporters of Juarez. The party is ambushed but Trane and Erin ensure that the Countess's carriage is safe. She informs them that she is transporting a shipment of gold and offers to steal it and share the proceeds with the Americans. Nina too has her designs on the gold as being invaluable to the rebel cause. Overhearing the various plottings, the Marquis de Labordère flees with the gold seeking the security of a nearby fort.

Trane and Erin storm the fort and recover the gold. Trane has been persuaded that the gold rightfully belongs to all the people but Erin violently disagrees and, in the final showdown, Erin is killed. Trane has made a commitment to Nina and the forces of Juarez.

COMMENT:
The initial critical response to *Vera Cruz* was disheartening, with strong reservations expressed over the blood, brutality and amorality. In essence a rollicking good Western had been made whose attitudes were probably ahead of the times.

64

Gary Cooper *(Photo: Flora Productions)*

Lancaster had personally promoted the idea of Gary Cooper as his co-star and would happily tell anyone of his belief that Coop's presence had added an extra two million dollars to the film's profits. The expensive production had been filmed on locations in Mexico and marked Lancaster's second consecutive collaboration with Robert Aldrich. During the early sixties Aldrich attempted to interest Lancaster in his projected film of *Taras Bulba*, commitments elsewhere prevented his involvement, and it would be almost twenty years before they were reunited professionally.

'Burt Lancaster, with a derisive smile which alone would make the movie worth a visit if you like smiles, throws a great deal of energy into making himself dangerously likeable.'

Saturday Review

THE KENTUCKIAN

(USA 1955)

RUNNING TIME: 101 minutes

Hecht-Lancaster Productions

CAST: Burt Lancaster (Big Eli), Dianne Foster (Hannah), Diana Lynn (Susie), John McIntire (Zack), Una Merkel (Sophie), Walter Matthau (Bodine), Donald MacDonald (Little Eli), John Carradine (Fletcher), John Litel (Babson), Rhys Williams (Constable)

DIRECTOR: Burt Lancaster
PRODUCER: Harold Hecht
SCREENPLAY: A.B. Guthrie Jr. from the novel *The Gabriel Horn* by Felix Holt.
ART DIRECTOR: Edward S. Haworth
DIRECTOR OF PHOTOGRAPHY: Ernest Laszlo
EDITOR: William B. Murphy
SOUND: John Kean and Paul Schmutz
MUSIC: Roy Webb
COSTUME: Norma

PLOT SYNOPSIS:

Widower Eli Wakefield, a backwoodsman in the Kentucky of the 1820s, is growing restless and decides to seek fresh pastures by travelling to Texas with his son, Little Eli. He is very weary too of the on-going family feud between himself and members of the Fromes clan. However, Eli is arrested by a village constable and the Fromes Brothers are informed of his whereabouts. Hannah, an indentured serving-girl at the local inn, helps Eli to escape and he repays her kindness by using his savings to buy her freedom. He invites Hannah to travel with them to Texas.

The trio stop in the village of Humility seeking to replenish their finances before journeying on. Hannah goes to work at an inn while Eli's brother Zack, a tobacco merchant, helps him find a job and introduces him to Susie, a local school teacher. Eli is lulled into changing his mind and accepting the possibility of a settled family life in Kentucky.

At work Hannah is viciously treated by the bullying innkeeper, Bodine. Soon Eli and Bodine clash and the latter is defeated in a whip duel. Resentful, Bodine calls in the Fromes brothers who kidnap Hannah and Little Eli and prepare an ambush. In the fight that follows both the Fromes brothers and Bodine are killed. Eli is now firmly determined to seek out the new lands of Texas and leaves by river boat with Hannah and Little Eli.

COMMENT:

Lancaster's first film as a director was shot on picturesque locations in Kentucky and Indiana. He admitted to having overtaxed himself in attempting the dual function of acting and directing, nonetheless he produced an agreeable, folksy Western. The film was invited to the Venice Film Festival and continues to highlight Lancaster's encouragement of new talent – stage actor Walter Matthau here makes his film début as the villain.

(Photo: Hecht-Lancaster Productions)

The Kentuckian was cut by four minutes before being shown in British cinemas. The censor had objected to the violence of the bull-whip sequence and to other segments, including one where a man is bludgeoned with a rifle butt. The critics were unanimous in their approval of the censor's actions.

'The good script, moreover, has good direction, and the credit goes to actor Lancaster. In his first attempt to run a whole show, he demonstrates a refreshing preference for natural setting and a remarkably pretty wit.'

Time

THE ROSE TATTOO

(USA 1955)

RUNNING TIME: 114 minutes

Hal Wallis Production for Paramount

CAST: Anna Magnani (Serafina Delle Rose), Burt Lancaster (Alvaro Mangia-cavallo), Marisa Pavan (Rosa Delle Rose), Ben Cooper (Jack Hunter), Virginia Grey (Estelle Hohengarten), Jo Van Fleet (Bessie), Sandro Giglio (Father De Leo)

DIRECTOR: Daniel Mann
PRODUCER: Hal B. Wallis
SCREENPLAY: Tennessee Williams from his play
PRODUCTION DESIGNERS: Hal Pereira and Tambi Larsen
DIRECTOR OF PHOTOGRAPHY: James Wong Howe
EDITOR: Warren Low
SOUND: Harold Lewis and Gene Garvin
MUSIC: Alex North

PLOT SYNOPSIS:

Serafina Delle Rosa, a volatile Sicilian woman living in the Italian quarter of a Gulf coast town, believes herself to have the perfect marriage. She idolises her virile, truck-driving husband unaware of his human failings of infidelity and crookedness. The rose tattoo imprinted on his chest is symbolic of their love, and Serafina has a passion for anything with the colour or scent of roses.

Following her husband's death she is grief-stricken and cuts herself off from the outside world. She lets herself go, becoming slovenly and irritable and convinced that all men are unspeakable. Serafina even objects to her daughter Rosa's engagement to a sailor. Her world is further shattered when a gossiping neighbour tells her that her husband was unfaithful. Hot-headed and near hysteria she attempts to force the truth from her local priest who protects himself by invoking the sanctity of the confessional.

It is in this fiery, feisty mood that she meets Alvaro Mangiacavallo, an oafish, muscular truck driver with a rose tattoo on his chest who revives vivid memories of her husband. Initially she rejects his rough advances but he gradually ingratiates himself by clowning, dancing and playing the buffoon to amuse her. She eventually succumbs to his charms. Having found happiness with Alvaro she now accepts her daughter's engagement and begins to look and live like the sunny Serafina of yore.

COMMENT:

Hal Wallis had purchased the screen rights to *The Rose Tattoo* with two built-in conditions; firstly, that Tennessee Williams himself would write the screenplay and, secondly, that Anna Magnani would star. Williams had written the play with her in mind but her tentative command of English had prevented her from appearing on stage. As with *Come Back Little Sheba* Lancaster was attracted by the acting challenge and he also provided some assurance of box-office success.

Anna Magnani   (Photo: Hal Wallis Production)

The film won three Academy Awards, including the Best Actress of 1955 for Magnani. During 1956 *The Rose Tattoo* was listed as the sixteenth American box-office winner with four million two hundred thousand dollars in rentals.

'Mr Lancaster, a much better actor than a few years ago one had any reason to suppose, contributes much of the boobyish sympathy and gentleness which the rôle needs.'

The Sunday Times

'Mr Lancaster's versatility grows more impressive with every film he makes.'

Tribune

TRAPEZE

(USA 1956)
RUNNING TIME: 106 minutes

Hecht-Lancaster Productions

CAST: Burt Lancaster (Mike Ribble), Tony Curtis (Tino Orsini), Gina Lollobrigida (Lola), Katy Jurado (Rosa), Thomas Gomez (Bouglione), Johnny Puleo (Max), Minor Watson (John Ringling-North), Gerard Landry (Chikki),J.P. Kerrien (Otto), Sidney James (Snake Man), Gabrielle Fonten (Old Woman)

DIRECTOR: Carol Reed
PRODUCER: James Hill
SCREENPLAY: James Webb
ART DIRECTOR: Rino Mondellini
DIRECTOR OF PHOTOGRAPHY: Robert Krasker
EDITOR: Bert Bates
MUSIC: Malcolm Arnold
COSTUMES: Frank Salvi and Gladys De Segonzac.

PLOT SYNOPSIS:

Tino Orsini, a brash young American acrobat, arrives at the Cirque Bouglione. He seeks out Mike Ribble, his father's former partner, and attempts to persuade him into becoming his trainer and mentor. In particular he wants Mike to teach him the dangerous aerial triple somersault. Mike, crippled from a fall, agrees to be his catcher and teach him the movement.

Tino learns quickly and a successful partnership begins to develop. Lola, a beautiful but scheming tumbler, attempts to break into the act using her feminine wiles on Tino. There are tensions in the relationship before Lola realises that she really loves Mike. She continues to use Tino to further her career much to Mike's disgust. He determines to expose her exploitation of Tino but resists when he realises that he loves Lola too. When Tino learns of their love he refuses to perform with Mike.

Mike is well aware of Tino's dependence on him to perform the triple somersault. When an American impressario come to the circus talent-scouting, Mike substitutes for Tino's catcher and, despite their mutual dislike, Tino manages a perfect triple. Tino has achieved his ambition and seems set for a successful circus career. He can forgive Mike who quietly slips away with Lola leaving Tino in the limelight.

COMMENT:

Trapeze, the realisation of Lancaster's long time ambition to make a circus film, was made on the most expensive budget of all the Hecht-Lancaster productions. Various press reports put Tony Curtis's salary at one hundred and fifty thousand dollars with Gina Lollobrigida receiving fifty thousand pounds and around one hundred thousand dollars spent on the script. All the money lavished on the production paid off, *Trapeze* was number three at the American box-office in 1956 taking seven and a half million dollars and Burt Lancaster made the first of his two appearances in the list of the year's top ten box-office stars.

(Photo: Hecht-Lancaster Productions) Gina Lollobrigida and Tony Curtis

The technical adviser on *Trapeze* was Eddie Ward from the Ringling Brothers Circus. He worked with Lollobrigida and Curtis to cut the amount of doubling to a minimum although he did double for Lancaster in some of the more dangerous moments. The two had previously worked together in 1935. Production was completed at the Cirque d'Hiver in France.

'*Trapeze* is an exciting, engrossing and original motion picture.'
Hollywood Reporter

'*Trapeze* is high-flying screen entertainment equipped with everything necessary to attract . . . circus thrills and excitement, a well-handled romantic triangle and a cast of potent marquee names.'
Variety

THE RAINMAKER

(USA 1956)

RUNNING TIME: 122 minutes

Hal Wallis Production for Paramount

CAST: Burt Lancaster (Starbuck), Katharine Hepburn (Lizzie Curry), Wendell Corey (Deputy File), Lloyd Bridges (Noah Curry), Earl Holliman (Jimmy Curry), Cameron Prud'homme (H.C. Curry), Yvonne Lime (Snookie Maguire), Wallace Ford (Sheriff)

DIRECTOR: Joseph Anthony
PRODUCER: Hal Wallis
SCREENPLAY: N. Richard Nash from his play
ART DIRECTORS: Hal Pereira and Walter Tyler
DIRECTOR OF PHOTOGRAPHY: Charles Lang Jr.
EDITOR: Warren Low
SOUND: Harold Lewis and Winston Leverett
MUSIC: Alex North
COSTUMES: Edith Head

PLOT SYNOPSIS:

1913. Kansas faces a crippling drought made worse by the burning summer heat. Land has dried up and cattle are dying. Into the state comes Starbuck, an itinerant, supremely confident con man, medicine man and self-styled rainmaker. He promises the good people of the area that he can provide their parched land with rain for a mere hundred dollar fee.

Whilst waiting for the citizens to make their choice Starbuck rests at the farmhouse of the Curry family, father H.C., sons Noah and Jimmy and spinster daughter Lizzie. Starbuck may be a phoney as a salesman but he has a genuine understanding of the family problems. He notices the way that Noah dominates the group, resenting Jimmy's girlfriend Snookie and causing much unpleasantness. He particularly sympathises with Lizzie; desperate for marriage, but convinced that she lacks looks and personality and ashamed by her family's faltering attempts to partner her with File, the deputy Sheriff. Starbuck's presence has a dynamic effect on the family; the father asserts his position and hires Starbuck as a rainmaker; Jimmy stands up to his brother, and Lizzie blossoms under his loving attention. He asks Lizzie to leave with him. File arrives to arrest Starbuck for conning the people of Kansas but is persuaded to let him go. Lizzie is attracted by Starbuck's mercurial, dazzling personality but sees her future with File.

Driving away from the farm a sudden storm ends the long drought. Starbuck chooses to see this as a sign that his powers have worked their magic.

COMMENT:

With *The Rainmaker* Hal Wallis continued his successful policy of adapting Broadway hits into films. Richard Nash's play had run for three and a half months during the 1954-55 Broadway season and Hollywood had paid a reputed three hundred and fifty thousand dollars for the screen rights.

Katharine Hepburn   *(Photo: Hal Wallis Production)*

Unlike *Come Back Little Sheba* and *The Rose Tattoo* the female character in *The Rainmaker* was not so dominant and a more even-handed two header was presented with Lancaster top-billed over veteran Oscar-winner Katherine Hepburn.

'He has done nothing better than this.'

Daily Herald

'Burt Lancaster too scores in this film, revealing acting talent which has been hidden in less worthy parts.'

Evening News

'Lancaster's Rainmaker is a highly persuasive charlatan. I half-believed he was responsible for the wet pavements which greeted me outside the theatre.'

Star

GUNFIGHT AT THE OK CORRAL

(USA 1957)
RUNNING TIME: 122 minutes

Hal Wallis Production

CAST: Burt Lancaster (Wyatt Earp), Kirk Douglas (Doc Holliday), Rhonda Fleming (Laura Denbow), Jo Van Fleet (Kate Fisher), John Ireland (Ringo), Lyle Bettger (Ike Clanton), Frank Faylen (Cotton Wilson), Earl Holliman (Charles Bassett), Ted De Corsia (Shanghai Pierce), Dennis Hopper (Billy Clanton)

DIRECTOR: John Sturges
PRODUCER: Hal B. Wallis
SCREENPLAY: Leon Uris from the article *The Killer* by George Scullin
ART DIRECTORS: Hal Pereira and Walter Tyler
DIRECTOR OF PHOTOGRAPHY: Charles B. Lang
EDITOR: Warren Low
SOUND: Harold Lewis and Gene Garvin
MUSIC: Dmitri Tiomkin

PLOT SYNOPSIS:
    1881. Wyatt Earp, dedicated marshal of Dodge City, is in Fort Griffin, Texas during the trial of the outlaws Johnnie Ringo and Ike Clanton. Earp helps save the life of Doc Holliday, a consumptive, professional gambler and accomplished gunslinger who was about to have met his death at the hands of a lynching mob. They return to Dodge City and Holliday evens the score when he helps Earp in a gun battle with three bank robbers. Earp is considering retiring as marshal and settling down as a rancher with Laura Denbow, a woman gambler whom he loves. However, he receives an urgent letter from his brother Virgil, who is the marshal of Tombstone in Arizona. Virgil needs his assistance to combat the Clanton-Ringo gang who are terrorising the town and its inhabitants. Laura begs him not to go but, accompanied by Holliday, he sets off for Tombstone.
    In Tombstone Johnny Earp is killed by the Clantons and Wyatt disregards his badge of office to challenge the Clantons to a showdown. Doc Holliday joins the Earps and, on 16 October 1881, the famous gunfight at the OK Corral takes place. The Clantons are all killed and, once again, Doc Holliday's intervention saves Wyatt Earp's life. Justice has been done.

COMMENT:
    In an interview some twenty years later Lancaster declared; 'I didn't want to do the picture at first. It was too much of a talkie! Too much dialogue in the script. The picture is about two men of action, Doc Holliday and Wyatt Earp. Men of few words, men who wouldn't have gone around intellectualising about their lives. I did the picture because Hal Wallis made me a promise that if I did *Corral* he would let me do *The Rainmaker* which really interested me.'

Kirk Douglas, Lancaster, John Hudson, De Forest Kelley *(Photo: Hal Wallis Production)*

The classic confrontation had been previously filmed in John Ford's *My Darling Clementine* and in this version the gunfight, which occupies five minutes on screen, took forty-four hours to choreograph and film.

The film was number twelve in the American chart taking some four million three hundred thousand dollars in 1957. This was Lancaster's final commitment for Hal Wallis and the two have never worked together since.

'Burt Lancaster is excellent as Wyatt and Kirk Douglas equally good as the drunken Doc Holliday.'

Evening News

'Burt Lancaster gives his greatest performance ever.'

Daily Mirror

SWEET SMELL OF SUCCESS

(USA 1957)

RUNNING TIME: 93 minutes

Hecht-Hill-Lancaster Productions

CAST: Burt Lancaster (J.J. Hunsecker), Tony Curtis (Sidney Falco), Susan Harrison (Susan Hunsecker), Marty Milner (Steve Dallas), Sam Levene (Frank D'Angelo), Barbara Nichols (Rita), Jeff Donnell (Sally), Joseph Leon (Robard), Edith Atwater (Mary), Emile Meyer (Harry Kello), Joe Frisco (Herbie Temple)

DIRECTOR: Alexander Mackendrick
PRODUCER: James Hill
EXECUTIVE PRODUCER: Harold Hecht
SCREENPLAY: Clifford Odets and Ernest Lehman
ART DIRECTOR: Edward Carrere
DIRECTOR OF PHOTOGRAPHY: James Wong Howe
EDITOR: Alan Crosland Jr.
SOUND: Jack Solomon
MUSIC: Elmer Bernstein

PLOT SYNOPSIS:

J.J. Hunsecker of the *Globe* is the most powerful columnist in New York; a ruthless, calculating man who cares for no-one except his nineteen year old sister. Susie. Sidney Falco is a young, unscrupulous press agent dependent on the likes of Hunsecker to publicise his clients. For five days Hunsecker has cut Falco from his column as a punishment. Falco was entrusted to break up the romance between Susie and guitar-player Steve Dallas, a man Hunsecker deems unworthy of his sister. Falco has failed and now the couple are planning marriage.

With Hunsecker's complicity Falco works on a plan to end the romance permanently. A smear is printed in a rival column that Dallas is both a communist and involved in drugs; he is immediately sacked by the Elysian Nightclub. Falco persuades Hunsecker to intervene and arrange Dallas's reinstatement, aware that the musician's pride will not allow him to accept the favour.

Meeting during rehearsals for Hunsecker's TV show *It's a Wonderful World*, Falco goads Dallas into rejecting Hunsecker's help. Aware of the scheming around him Dallas vilifies Hunsecker as a national disgrace. Susie promises never to see Dallas again. However Hunsecker has been personally insulted and exacts his revenge. Falco frames Dallas on a drugs charge and is rewarded with the assurance that he will write Hunsecker's column whilst J.J. is on holiday.

Triumphant, Falco is summoned to Hunsecker's apartment. J.J. is not to be seen but Susie is and threatens suicide to undermine Falco's new-found status with her brother. When J.J. arrives he finds Falco and Susie in a seemingly compromising situation and is outraged. He frees Dallas and implicates Falco in the drugs case. Falco is arrested. Meanwhile Susie finally stands up for herself and leaves home for Dallas. J.J. has been defeated.

Tony Curtis   *(Photo: Hecht-Hill-Lancaster Productions)*

COMMENT:

Sweet Smell of Success represents the kind of serious challenging cinema to which Lancaster increasingly chose to commit himself. His performance is a studious character study and the film marked a remarkable American début for British director Alexander Mackendrick whose previous credits had come largely from Ealing Studios and had included *The Ladykillers* and *The Man in the White Suit*.

The film did not do well at the box-office much to Lancaster's disappointment and was the first substantial failure for Hecht-Lancaster Productions. Hecht had not expected the film to do well and was proved right.

'Lancaster, his cold eyes enlarged to inhuman size by magnifying spectacles is magnificent and horrific.'

News Chronicle

'Burt Lancaster is so heavily sinister he could at any moment have whipped off his glasses and revealed himself as a Nazi spy.'

Sunday Express

RUN SILENT, RUN DEEP

(USA 1958)
RUNNING TIME: 93 minutes

Hecht-Hill-Lancaster Productions

CAST: Clark Gable (Cmdr. Richardson), Burt Lancaster (Lt. Jim Bledsoe), Jack Warden (Mueller), Brad Dexter (Cartwright), Don Rickles (Ruby), Nick Cravat (Russo), Hoe Maross (Kohler), Mary La Roche (Laura), Eddie Foy III (Larto), Rudy Bond (Cullen)

DIRECTOR: Robert Wise
PRODUCER: Harold Hecht
ASSOCIATE PRODUCER: William Schorr
SCREENPLAY: John Gay from the novel by Edward L. Beach
ART DIRECTOR: Edward Carrere
DIRECTOR OF PHOTOGRAPHY: Russell Harlan
EDITOR: George Boemler
SOUND: Fred Hall
MUSIC: Franz Waxman

PLOT SYNOPSIS:
1942. During war service Commander Richardson's submarine is sunk by a Japanese Akikaze destroyer in the treacherous Bongo Straits. Subsequently Richardson is re-assigned to command the USS *Nerka* and given another mission in the same area of conflict. He finds his new command less than welcoming; it has generally been expected by the crew and the officer himself that the popular Lieutenant Bledsoe would have gained the promotion to commander. Bledsoe's disappointment borders on mutiny but he is respectful of the older officer.
    Obsessed by his desire to claim vengeance on the Japanese destroyer Richardson relentlessly drills the men in special attack training. He is successful when they torpedo a Japanese destroyer and attack a convoy in the Bongo Straits. Richardson is beginning to have nightmares and defies campaign orders when an opportunity arises to attack a destroyer that he has sought. The battle is now a contest of wills between Richardson and an enemy destroyer and submarine. When Richardson is injured, Bledsoe takes command and sinks the destroyer. The submarine surfaces and is attacked by planes, Richardson dies but he has the knowledge that his colleagues' deaths have not gone unmarked. Bledsoe and the crew pay silent tribute to Richardson, a man they have grown to admire.

COMMENT:
Run Silent, Run Deep marked a return to a more commercial fare for Lancaster's company after the disappointing returns from *Sweet Smell of Success*. James Hill had acted as producer on *Sweet Smell of Success*, a long-time story consultant for Lancaster, he was now made a full partner in the company henceforward known as Hecht-Hill-Lancaster Productions.
    Clark Gable was signed and top-billed, with the author of the original novel, Captain Edward L. Beach, hired as a technical adviser.

Clark Gable

(Hecht-Hill-Lancaster Productions)

'It's a taut, superbly conceived piece of film craft. Two of Hollywood's real dependables, Clark Gable and Burt Lancaster, are the mainspring.'
News of the World

'While Clark Gable and Burt Lancaster have no chance of doing great things, convincing and competent they certainly are.'
Evening Standard

'Some good sea fights. Otherwise it's damn the torpedoes, half-speed ahead.'
Time

SEPARATE TABLES

(USA 1958)

RUNNING TIME: 98 minutes

Clifton Productions for Hecht-Hill-Lancaster Productions

CAST: Deborah Kerr (Sybil Railton-Bell), Rita Hayworth (Ann Shankland), David Niven (Major Pollock), Wendy Hiller (Miss Cooper), Burt Lancaster (John Malcolm), Gladys Cooper (Mrs Railton-Bell), Cathleen Nesbitt (Lady Matheson), Felix Aylmer (Mr Fowler), Rod Taylor (Charles)

DIRECTOR: Delbert Mann
PRODUCER: Harold Hecht
SCREENPLAY: Terence Rattigan and John Gay from Rattigan's play
ART DIRECTOR: Edward Carrere
DIRECTOR OF PHOTOGRAPHY: Charles Lang Jr.
EDITORS: Marjorie Fowler and Charles Ennis
SOUND: Fred Lau
MUSIC: David Raksin
COSTUMES: Edith Head

PLOT SYNOPSIS:

The Beauregarde Hotel, Bournemouth. In one night at this drab seaside resort hotel two separate events come to a head. The glamorous Ann Malcolm arrives to visit her former husband, John Malcolm, a heavy-drinking American writer who is attempting to rebuild his life. At one point in their marriage he had attempted to murder her and has served time in prison. Malcolm finds her re-appearance extremely annoying as he is about to be engaged to the hotel proprietress Miss Cooper. Miss Cooper soon realises how much the former husband and wife need each other. Despite her poise and sophistication Ann shares the same fear of loneliness and growing old. With Miss Cooper's self-sacrificing assistance their reconciliation is achieved.

Amongst the other hotel residents are the bluff Major Pollock who regales people with accounts of his war record and the timid, dowdy Sybil who is hopelessly dominated by her mother Mrs Railton-Bell. On this evening the major is revealed as a phoney, his service record a lie. He has just been arrested for annoying women in the local cinema. Mrs Railton-Bell insists that the major is asked to leave the hotel at once. Sybil and the major have struck up a tentative friendship and through each other's concern find courage. The major decides to stay at the hotel and face his possible ostracisation by the other guests. At breakfast next morning Sybil defies her mother for the first time and talks to the major. They have achieved a small victory in facing the world together.

COMMENT:

Separate Tables had run successfully on Broadway in 1956 with Margaret Leighton and Eric Portman playing the dual rôles in this largely four-handed encounter. Lancaster's company bought the screen rights on condition that Terence Rattigan would write the screenplay. Laurence Olivier was hired to direct and co-star with his wife Vivien Leigh thus filling two of the rôles.

(Photo: Clifton Productions)

During preparations for filming Lancaster and Olivier clashed, ostensibly over the playing of the character of John Malcolm, although it was reported that Olivier had only agreed to direct if Spencer Tracy was cast in the part. Olivier was replaced as director and David Niven and Rita Hayworth, the wife of James Hill, filled the rôles vacated by the Oliviers.

The film won two Academy Awards; Best Actor for Niven and Best Supporting Actress for Wendy Hiller, and was listed as twentieth in the American chart of box-office winners in 1959 with two million seven hundred thousand dollars to its credit.

'Burt Lancaster powerfully suggests the tensions and violence locked up in a man fundamentally tolerant and good.'

Daily Telegraph

THE DEVIL'S DISCIPLE

(United Kingdon 1959)
RUNNING TIME: 82 minutes

A co-production of Hecht-Hill-Lancaster and Brynaprod

CAST: Burt Lancaster (Anthony Anderson), Kirk Douglas (Richard Dudgeon), Laurence Olivier (General Burgoyne), Janette Scott (Judith Anderson), Eva LeGallienne (Mrs Dudgeon), Harry Andrews (Major Swindon), Basil Sydney (Lawyer Hawkins), George Rose (British Sergeant), Neil McCallum (Christopher Dudgeon)

DIRECTOR: Guy Hamilton
PRODUCER: Harold Hecht
SCREENPLAY: John Dighton and Roland Kibbee from the play by G.B. Shaw
PRODUCTION DESIGNER: Terrence Verity and Edward Carrere
DIRECTOR OF PHOTOGRAPHY: Jack Hildyard
EDITOR: Alan Osbiston
SOUND: Leslie Hammond
PRODUCTION MANAGER: Gilbert Kurland
MUSIC: Richard Rodney Bennett
COSTUMES: Mary Grant

PLOT SYNOPSIS:
New Hampshire, 1777, during the War of Independence. Under the urbane leadership of General ('Gentleman Johnny') Burgoyne, British forces marching from Canada take over the small town of Springtown. To quell the desire for resistance amongst the colonists a town notable Timothy Dudgeon, is hanged.

Dudgeon's son Dick is determined to avenge his father's murder and contemptuous of any colonist who acquiesces in the British occupation. The stern village pastor Anthony Anderson of neighbouring Westbridge is sympathetic to Dudgeon's cause but worried by his wife Judith's growing attraction to the rebel.

Burgoyne chooses to hang another citizen as an example, pastor Anderson is to be the victim. When the troops arrive at the Anderson household they encounter Dudgeon who is mistakenly assumed to be the pastor. Anderson meanwhile has fled to join the revolutionary forces. Enjoying the jape Dudgeon doesn't resist arrest and is sentenced to hang, much to the despair of Judith.

The pastor intercepts a message intended for Burgoyne and, fighting off the British troops, bargains for Dudgeon's life, saving the rebel and thereby regaining his wife's affections.

Ever-civilised, Burgoyne and Dudgeon have tea together and it is later discovered that the general and his troops surrendered at Saratoga three weeks afterwards.

COMMENT:
The rift between Lancaster and Laurence Olivier was quickly healed when Olivier agreed to appear in *The Devil's Disciple*, a co-production between Lancaster and Kirk Douglas.

(Photo: Hecht-Hill-Lancaster and Brynaprod)

In his preface to the text George Bernard Shaw wrote; 'The Devil's Disciple does not contain a single even passably novel incident.' Shaw had disliked the work and refused to let the play be staged in Britain, thus the first production was in America.

The seven hundred and fifty thousand pound production had a fairly troubled history; economics dictated a tight shooting schedule and the original director Alexander Mackendrick, was sacked for working too slowly. Lancaster admitted that the footage shot by Mackendrick was the best in the film but that the budget did not run to his time-consuming meticulousness. The production manager was also replaced during filming. The original adverts ran: 'Burt, Kirk and Larry are coming – by George!'

'Burt Lancaster, though too young-looking, makes a splendid pastor, especially in his metamorphosis from sober man of the cloth to fierce rebel soldier.'
Daily Worker

THE UNFORGIVEN

(USA 1960)
RUNNING TIME: 125 minutes

James Productions and Hecht-Hill-Lancaster

CAST: Audrey Hepburn (Rachel), Burt Lancaster (Ben Zachary), Audie Murphy (Cash), Lillian Gish (Mattilda), Doug McClure (Andy), Charles Bickford (Zeb Rawlins), Joseph Wiseman (Abe Kelsey), John Saxon (Johnny Portugal), Albert Salmi (Charlie Rawlins), June Walker (Hagar Rawlins)

DIRECTOR: John Huston
PRODUCER : James Hill
SCREENPLAY: Ben Maddow from the novel by Alan le May
PRODUCTION DESIGNER: Stephen Grimes
DIRECTOR OF PHOTOGRAPHY: Franz Planer
EDITOR: Hugh Russell Lloyd
SOUND: Basil Fenton Smith
PRODUCTION MANAGER: Gilber Kurland
MUSIC: Dmitri Tiomkin
COSTUMES: Dorothy Jeakins

PLOT SYNOPSIS:
Texas. Ben Zachary, leader of the Zachary family since the death of his father in a Kiowa Indian attack, is in partnership with the Rawlins family, cattle-ranching. One day, Abe Kelsey, an embittered veteran of the Civil War, rides through the area spreading the news that Rachel, Ben's adopted sister is a Kiowa Indian who was rescued from a massacre and fostered. This gossip is strongly denied.

When the Rawlins' oldest boy Charlie is killed by the Kiowa after courting Rachel, Kelsey again states his charge. Rawlins wants Rachel handed over to the Kiowas, who are led by Johnny Portugal. Ben refuses to let her be examined and Rawlins dissolves the partnership. Ben asks his mother, Mattilda, whether there is any substance to the rumours. Mattilda informs him that Rachel is a Kiowa Indian and that her real brother is Portugal. Ben's brother Cash leaves the family; his hatred of the Kiowa more powerful than his love for Rachel. Ben and the rest of the family, isolated by the community, must fight the Kiowa attacks alone.

Rachel attempts to return to her people and save the Zacharys but Ben is determined to stand and face the Indians. In subsequent skirmishes Mattilda is killed and the youngest Zachary, Andy, is wounded. However, Rachel affirms her allegiance to the family when she kills Portugal.

Cash's conscience cannot permit him to stay away. Returning to the family Cash and the others fight off the remaining Kiowa. Although the homestead has been destroyed, the family are united, with Ben and Rachel resolved to marry.

COMMENT:
The Unforgiven was filmed on a budget variously reported as between three and a half and five and a half million dollars in the mining town of Durango in Mexico. Tony Curtis was originally set for the rôle played by Audie Murphy.

(Photo: James Productions and Hecht-Hill-Lancaster) Audrey Hepburn

Because of his lack of involvement in the script and the fact that he did not retain the final say over the released film, John Huston claims that 'at best it's an adopted child,'

During filming there was something of a jinx on the production; Audrey Hepburn was thrown from a white Arab stallion and needed a month to recover, Audie Murphy was involved in a serious boating accident and three technicians were killed in a 'plane crash.

'If Burt Lancaster's performance is no more than picturesque, it is because Ben Zachary is a stock character. What more can an actor do with a strong silent man except be beautifully strong and silent?'

Daily Telegraph

ELMER GANTRY

(USA 1960)

RUNNING TIME: 145 minutes

Elmer Gantry Productions

CAST: Burt Lancaster (Elmer Gantry), Jean Simmons (Sister Sharon Falconer), Arthur Kennedy (Jim Lefferts), Shirley Jones (Lulu Bains), Dean Jagger (William L. Morgan), Patti Page (Sister Rachel), Edward Andrews (George Babbitt), John McIntire (Rev. Pengilly), Joe Maross (Pete)

DIRECTOR: Richard Brooks
PRODUCER: Bernard Smith
SCREENPLAY: Richard Brooks from the novel by Sinclair Lewis.
ART DIRECTOR: Edward Carrere
DIRECTOR OF PHOTOGRAPHY: John Alton
EDITOR: Margie Fowler
SOUND: Harry Mills
MUSIC: Andre Previn
COSTUMES: Dorothy Jeakins

PLOT SYNOPSIS:

Elmer Gantry is a born con man with the gift of the gab and a strongly extrovert personality. When he is dismissed from a theological college for seducing the deacon's daughter he takes to the road as a travelling salesman. He hustles for a living as a saloon gambler but gives a quick display of his oratory and charm when he persuades the patrons of one pub to part with their money for two Salvation Army girls collecting at Christmas time. Drifting along he attends the revival meetings of Sister Sharon Falconer. Attracted by Sharon he charms his way onto her staff and joins the wandering troupe of singers and musicians.

Sharon's quiet, sincere style and Gantry's fire and brimstone spellbinding make a surefire combination and the troupe signs for a week of meetings in the city of Zenith. In Zenith a newspaperman attacks the entire revivalist movement and a spiteful prostitute, Lulu Bains, frames Gantry by issuing compromising photographs to the press. She later retracts the story but Gantry's public image is tarnished and outraged citizens wreck one meeting.

Sharon and Gantry fall in love but the Sister is unwilling to give up what she regards as her mission in life. Sharon continues to work on building the Tabernacle which will be her headquarters. On opening night she miraculously cures a deaf man. On the same evening the Tabernacle is burnt to the ground and Sharon is engulfed in the flames. Gantry goes back on the road.

COMMENT:

Elmer Gantry was an ideal part for Burt Lancaster – a charming, forceful con man, loquacious and brimming with personality. He admitted; 'Some parts you fall into like an old glove. Elmer really wasn't acting. It was me.'

Frustrated at his attempts to capture a treatment of *Elmer Gantry* since 1947, Richard Brooks had eventually bought the rights to the novel and spent two years developing the script. Lancaster won the Golden Globe award as Best Actor in a

Edward Andrews   *(Photo: Elmer Gantry Productions)*

drama, his second New York Critics Award as Best Actor and, on his second nomination, the Academy Award as Best Actor of 1960. The film won a total of three Academy Awards; with Shirley Jones chosen as Best Supporting Actress and Richard Brooks voted the Best Screenplay Award.

THE YOUNG SAVAGES

(USA 1961)

RUNNING TIME: 103 minutes

Contemporary Production

CAST: Burt Lancaster (Hank Bell), Dina Merrill (Karin Bell), Shelley Winters (Mary di Pace), Edward Andrews (Dan Cole), Vivian Nathan (Mrs Escalante), Larry Gates (Randolph), Telly Savalas (Lt. Richard Gunnison), Pilar Seurat (Louisa Escalante), Jody Fair (Angela Rugiello)

DIRECTOR: John Frankenheimer
PRODUCER: Pat Duggan
SCREENPLAY: Edward Anhalt and J.P. Miller from the novel by Evan Hunter, *A Matter of Conviction*
ART DIRECTOR: Burr Smidt
DIRECTOR OF PHOTOGRAPHY: Lionel Lindon
EDITOR: Edna Warren
SOUND: Harry Mills
PRODUCTION MANAGER: Gilbert Kurland
MUSIC: David Amram
COSTUMES: Jack Angel and Roselle Novello

PLOT SYNOPSIS:

New York's Spanish Harlem. In broad daylight the blind Roberto Escalante is murdered on the steps of his apartment by Reardon, Aposto and Danny di Pace, three members of an Italian gang. The gang are subsequently arrested by the police.

District Attorney, Daniel Cole, is running for Governor and views the case as of immeasurable political value in his campaign. He assigns his assistant, Hank Bell, to the case, stipulating that a conviction must be acquired. Bell is equally ambitious and his marriage to well-connected, wealthy socialite Karin has taken him far from his origins of an Italian slum upbringing in the very district where the murder was committed. Initially he sees the incident as an open and shut case with a conviction assured.

As the investigation progresses Bell discovers several disquieting facts; Escalante was in fact a decoy who concealed weapons for a rival gang and di Pace is the son of a woman he once loved. Bell faces conflicting pressures – from his wife and the press to show a sense of social responsibility and understanding of the life of these underprivileged youths and from his boss and Mrs Escalante to gain the conviction without the luxury of conscience.

At the trial, and regardless of personal repercussions, Bell finds extenuating circumstances and unveils the personal innocence of di Pace who had lied to protect other members of the gang. Bell has put a halt to his political rise but won the respect of his wife and established his integrity.

Chris Robinson *(Photo: Contemporary Production)*

COMMENT:

The Young Savages, based on actual events and filmed on New York locations, began Lancaster's association with the two directors who were to dominate his screen work during the sixties. It was his first film with John Frankenheimer, one of the generation of film-makers then emerging from the age of American live television. It was also during the making of *The Young Savages* that he met Sydney Pollack. Pollack was a friend of Frankenheimer's employed on the film as a dialogue director and acting coach. His ambition was to direct and Lancaster called Universal Studios to see if they had a training programme. They didn't, but instead allowed Pollack to be an observer for six months on a salary of one hundred dollars a week. He eventually directed Lancaster in *The Scalphunters* and *Castle Keep*.

'Mr Lancaster, far removed from the former muscleman forever swinging about the rigging of pirate ships, gives a performance of strength and stature to a film of strength and stature.'

Daily Mail

'The direction is fast and forceful and, if Mr Lancaster wears that habitual expression which makes him the first cousin to a bloodhound confused as to the trail, that is not through any lack of pace in the action or, indeed, to any weakness in Mr Lancaster's own performance.'

The Times

JUDGEMENT AT NUREMBERG

(USA 1961)
RUNNING TIME: 183 minutes

Roxlom Productions

CAST: Spencer Tracy (Judge Dan Haywood), Burt Lancaster (Ernst Janning),
Richard Widmark (Col. Tad Lawson), Marlene Dietrich (Mme. Bertholt),
Maximilian Schell (Hans Rolfe), Judy Garland (Irene Hoffman), Montgomery
Clift (Rudolf Petersen), Ed Binns (Senator Burkette), Werner Klemperer
(Emil Hahm)

DIRECTOR: Stanley Kramer
PRODUCER: Stanley Kramer
ASSOCIATE PRODUCER: Philip Langner
SCREENPLAY: Abby Mann
PRODUCTION DESIGNER: Rudolph Sternad
DIRECTOR OF PHOTOGRAPHY: Ernest Laszlo
EDITOR: Fred Knudtson
SOUND: James Speak
PRODUCTION MANAGER: Clem Beauchamp
MUSIC: Ernest Gold
COSTUMES: Joe King

PLOT SYNOPSIS:
1948. Four German judges are on trial in Nuremberg before American judge
Dan Haywood from Maine. They are charged with crimes against humanity; it is
claimed that by passing pro-Nazi laws in the 1930s they have woefully failed to
uphold the justice and liberty owing to every man. Three of the judges are fairly
minor figures but the fourth is Ernst Janning, once respected as one of the
foremost legal scholars in the world.
    Colonel Tad Lawson is the prosecuting attorney and, for the defence, is Hans
Rolfe. The two frequently clash in a case of bitter accusations and unpalatable
truths. Many witnesses are called who speak of the horrors of the Nazi atrocities;
Lawson screens footage of the concentrations camps and demands the maximum
penalty, Rolfe claims that the judges are only as guilty as the whole German
nation. Throughout the trial Janning remains impassive and unmoved by the
claims and counter-claims.
    Judge Haywood attempts to discover the nature of the German people and
spends his spare time wandering the city and conversing with widow Madame
Bertholt. Instinctively trusting Haywood, Janning requests a private meeting. As
the trial slowly grinds on Janning is aware of the increasing difficulty in coming to
any definite conclusions. In court Janning rises and makes a statement in which he
denounces himself and his fellow judges for the acts. He admits the futility of
attempting to rationalise acquiescence in acts of mass brutality and inhumanity.
His statement causes a controversy, the other judges are shocked and Rolfe is
disgusted, but it sums up the feelings of the court.

(Photo: Roxlom Productions) Torben Meyer

COMMENT:

Judgement at Nuremberg began life as a Playhouse 90 play for American television which the original writer, Abby Mann, adapted into a motion picture, practically doubling the length in the process.

Lancaster seemed a strange choice for the part of an elderly, cultured German judge. On television the rôle had been more comfortably filled by Paul Lukas and it had been rejected by Laurence Olivier on the eve of filming. Many scenes were shot on actual German locations.

The film won two Academy Awards; Maximilian Schell was chosen Best Actor and Abby Mann honoured for his screenplay.

'Montgomery Clift and Judy Garland, as two of the witnesses, and Burt Lancaster as a defendant, far surpass anything I have seen them do before.'

Show

BIRDMAN OF ALCATRAZ

(USA 1962)

RUNNING TIME: 147 minutes

Norma Productions

CAST: Burt Lancaster (Robert Stroud), Karl Malden (Harvey Shoemaker), Thelma Ritter (Elizabeth Stroud), Betty Field (Stella Johnson), Neville Brand (Bull Ransom), Edmond O'Brien (Tom Gaddis), Hugh Marlowe (Roy Comstock), Telly Savalas (Feto Gomez), Whit Bissell (Dr Ellis), Graham Denton (Kramer)

DIRECTOR: John Frankenheimer
PRODUCERS: Stuart Miller and Guy Trosper
SCREENPLAY: Guy Trosper from the book by Thomas E. Gaddis
ART DIRECTOR: Edward Carrere
DIRECTOR OF PHOTOGRAPHY: Burnett Guffey
EDITOR: Edward Mann
SOUND: George Cooper
MUSIC: Elmer Bernstein

PLOT SYNOPSIS:

In 1909 Robert Stroud is sentenced to twelve years imprisonment for murder. Later he forfeits his chance for parole by attacking a fellow prisoner. When Stroud's mother travels half the country to visit him and is refused permission Stroud erupts, killing a warder. Violent and unpredictable he is sentenced to death. However, his mother persuades the President to commute the sentence to life imprisonment in solitary confinement.

Walking in the exercise yard one day he rescues a sparrow and cares for it, eventually acquiring a canary and developing a strong interest in birds. His hobby humanises him and a wary friendship grows with his warder, Bull Ransom. Through dedicated study Stroud becomes a world authority on rare bird diseases and writes a text book. His growing renown brings widow-woman Stella Johnson to the prison and they go into business together, marketing bird medicines. When an attempt is made to deprive Stroud of his birds the authorities are publicly embarrassed into changing their decision by the marriage of Stella to Stroud and the ensuing newspaper publicity for his case.

Later Stroud is transferred to Alcatraz where he attempts to write a book on penology which is confiscated. He becomes a much respected elder to the other inmates. Thomas Gaddis, a journalist, becomes interested in the Stroud story and writes a book on his life. The two meet only once, in 1959, when Stroud is tranferred from Alcatraz to a federal prison hospital where he is to spend his last years.

COMMENT:

Birdman of Alcatraz began filming under director Charles Crichton in 1961 before *Judgement at Nuremberg*. Lancaster argued with the director and filming ceased after several weeks. Frankenheimer was called in as a replacement and production resumed after major script changes.

(Photo: Norma Productions)

Lancaster became obsessed with the life and times of Robert Stroud. Years later he said; 'I had a very strong, almost maniacal concern with the whole problem of penology. I did an enormous amount of reading, I talked to judges, I read every letter that Stroud wrote. When I would play scenes I would start to cry before they turned the camera. I couldn't control myself, I was so deeply involved.'

He received his third Academy Award nomination and was voted Best Foreign Actor by the British Academy.

'Frankenheimer, aided by an intelligently muted performance by Lancaster, achieves a compelling subtlety.'

Monthly Film Bulletin

A CHILD IS WAITING

(USA 1962)

RUNNING TIME: 104 minutes

Larcas Productions

CAST: Burt Lancaster (Dr Matthew Clark), Judy Garland (Jean Hansen), Gena Rowlands (Sophie Widdicombe), Steven Hill (Ted Widdicombe), Bruce Ritchey (Reuben Widdicombe), Gloria McGehee (Mattie), Paul Stewart (Goodman), Lawrence Tierney (Douglas Benham), Elizabeth Wilson (Miss Fogarty)

DIRECTOR: John Cassavetes
PRODUCER: Stanley Kramer
ASSOCIATE PRODUCER: Philip Langer
SCREENPLAY: Abby Mann
PRODUCTION DESIGNER: Rudolph Sternad
DIRECTOR OF PHOTOGRAPHY: Joseph La Shelle
EDITOR: Gene Fowler Jr.
SOUND: James L. Speak
PRODUCTION MANAGER: Nate Edwards
MUSIC: Ernest Gold

PLOT SYNOPSIS:

Jean Hansen, a single woman in her thirties, attempts to give her life some meaning and applies for a position at a State hospital for retarded children. She is employed by the unbending, stern Matthew Clark, the head of the hospital, who remains sceptical about her ability to work within his system of child care.

Jean sets to work, lavishing her affections on the children and becoming particularly involved in the case of Reuben Widdicombe, a child who resists all endeavours to make him participate in the life of the hospital. Jean believes that a visit from the boy's parents would be of enormous benefit but Clark refuses her permission to contact them. Undeterred, Jean meets Mrs Widdicombe who is now living with her second husband and a daughter. She admits that it was her domineering, maternal protectiveness which has led to Reuben's condition and is shamed into visiting him. At the visit she will not speak to her son who runs away from the hospital. He is brought back by Dr Clark.

Clark hopes that Jean has learned from the experience that one has to be firm and encourage the children to be independent, not just smother them with love. Reuben begins to come out of his shell and, encouraged by Jean, he plays a part in the hospital's Thanksgiving play. In the audience is Reuben's father Ted, now willing to support his son.

COMMENT:

A Child is Waiting was filmed at Pacific State Hospital in Pomona, California, and, with the exception of the leading child actor, all the juveniles were played by patients. Again the film was based on an Abby Mann television script from 1957 in which Lancaster's rôle had been played by Pat Hingle.

Judy Garland   (Photo: Larcas Productions)

The mix of big name Hollywood stars and a documentary style approach was not the easiest or most desirable to achieve. Director Cassavetes objected to the way in which the film had been sentimentalised after he had finished his work. In Britain the poor commercial prospects delayed the release of the film until 1966.

'Burt Lancaster is fine and convincing as the prototype of men who are working hard to bring progress and enlightenment in this dark field.'
Sunday Express
'Lancaster is excellent as the tough psychiatrist, battling for more money, battling to have his methods understood, battling his own failures.'
The Sun

THE LEOPARD

(USA/Italy 1962)
RUNNING TIME: 205 minutes

Titanus/SNPC/SGC for 20th Century Fox

CAST: Burt Lancaster (Don Fabrizio), Alain Delon (Tancredi), Claudia Cardinale (Angelica Sedara), Paolo Stoppa (Don Calogero Sedara), Rina Morelli (Maria Stella), Romolo Valli (Father Pirrone), Serge Reggiani (Don Ciccio Tumeo), Leslie French (Cavalier Chevally), Ivo Garrani (Col. Pallavicino)

DIRECTOR: Luchino Visconti
PRODUCER: Goffredo Lombardo
SCREENPLAY: Luchino Visconti and others from the novel by Guiseppe de Lampedusa
ART DIRECTOR: Mario Garbuglia
DIRECTOR OF PHOTOGRAPHY: Guiseppe Rotunno
EDITOR: Mario Serandrei
SOUND: Mario Messina
PRODUCTION MANAGERS: Enzo Provenzale and Giorgio Adriani
MUSIC: Nino Rota
COSTUMES: Piero Tosi
ORIGINAL LANGUAGE TITLE: Il Gattopardo

PLOT SYNOPSIS:
Sicily, the 1860s. Garibaldi is acting to unite the disparate provinces into an Italian state. Prince Don Fabrizio of Salina belongs to the old order of nobility but acknowledges that he must adapt to changing times and circumstances. His nephew, Tancredi, joins the fray and leaves the estate with his uncle's blessing. Order is restored and Tancredi returns to pass the balmy summer at the family's country retreat in Donna Fugata. The family is welcomed by the Mayor, Don Calogero, a prosperous merchant and a member of the rising middle class.

Fabrizio invites Calogero to dinner as a mark of his growing awareness of his position in the new order. At the feast Tancredi is strongly attracted to Calogero's daughter Angelica and, although the Prince's own daughter Concetta is in love with Tancredi, the Prince arranges a marriage. For the Prince it is a marriage of convenience, crossing the class barrier and providing a much needed deposit in the family coffers from Angelica's dowry.

Later the Prince is offered a seat in the Senate of his country but declines preferring to keep some distance between himself and the new rulers.

A grand aristocratic ball is held to herald Angelica's arrival into society but for the Prince it only awakens a bitter nostalgia for the better days of his youth. Wearied by age and the changing world the Prince has cause for further reflection when he hears four shots signifying the deaths of four traitors. He can only ponder his status as one among the last of a dying breed.

(Photo: Titanus/SNPC/SGC)

COMMENT:

Italian director Luchino Visconti had arranged a deal with 20th Century Fox to ensure financing for his costly epic. His original choice for the rôle of the Count was a famous Russian actor, Cherkasov, who was now too old. Second in line had been either Laurence Olivier or Marlon Brando. When neither actor was available Fox provided a short list of Spencer Tracy, Anthony Quinn or Lancaster. Initially against his better judgement Visconti chose Lancaster.

The film was a huge success on the Continent but flopped badly in Britain and America where the film was reduced from 70mm to 35mm, printed on inferior colour stock, cut by almost three quarters of an hour and poorly dubbed. Visconti disowned this version although Lancaster and Sydney Pollack had worked on the dubbing of the foreign version.

It remains one of Lancaster's personal favourites from amongst all his rôles. He has said; 'The Leopard was the best result for someone like me. When the Italians heard that I was going to play a Sicilian Prince they were very hostile towards me. "How dare this man play this part!" they said. But I proved to them I could do it. It was very pleasing to me.'

SEVEN DAYS IN MAY

(USA 1963)
RUNNING TIME: 120 minutes

A Seven Arts – Joel Production

CAST: Burt Lancaster (Gen. James M. Scott),Kirk Douglas (Col. Martin Casey), Fredric March (President Jordan Lyman), Ava Gardner (Eleanor Holbrook), Martin Balsam (Paul Girard), George Macready (Christopher Todd), Whit Bissell (Sen. Prentice), Hugh Marlowe (Harold McPherson), Richard Anderson (Col. Murdock), Andrew Duggan (Col. Henderson), John Houseman (Adm. Barnswell)

DIRECTOR: John Frankenheimer
PRODUCER: Edward Lewis
SCREENPLAY: Rod Serling from the novel by Fletcher Knebel and Charles W. Bailey II
PRODUCTION DESIGNER: Cary Odell
DIRECTOR OF PHOTOGRAPHY: Ellsworth Fredericks
EDITOR: Ferris Webster
SOUND: Joe Edmonson
PRODUCTION MANAGER: Hal Polaire
MUSIC: Jerry Goldsmith
COSTUMES: Wes Jeffries

PLOT SYNOPSIS:
In the White House President Lyman faces his lowest popularity rating. His nuclear disarmament treaty with Russia has polarised opinion within the country and the military where it is firmly opposed by General Scott. Scott sees Lyman's actions as criminally negligent and plots a military take-over of the country.

Scott's subordinate, Colonel Casey, begins to suspect a conspiracy; he is informed by a colleague of project Ecomcom, an unlisted base in El Paso authorised by Scott, and a right-wing Senator makes knowing references to a practice alert scheduled for the following Sunday. Casey confesses his fears to the President who is suitably convinced to send his closest aides in search of proof: Senator Clark is sent to discover the base in El Paso and Paul Girard is despatched to Gibraltar to obtain a confession from Admiral Barnswell, whom it is believed has backed out of the conspiracy. Casey is to wine and dine Eleanor Holbrook, Scott's former mistress, in an attempt to discover any incriminating papers. Clark uncovers the base but is held captive, Girard obtains the confession but is killed in an air crash *en route* however, Casey uncovers revealing letters owned by Holbrook.

As Sunday draws closer the President appeals to Scott's honour, he has no proof but asks for the resignation of Scott and his co-conspirators. Scott is contemptuous of the democratic process and refuses whilst Lyman will not sink to blackmail by using the Holbrook letters.

The President holds his press conference on the Sunday during which an embassy official arrives from Madrid with Admiral Barnswell's confession which

Kirk Douglas *(Photo: A Seven Arts – Joel Production)*

has been discovered amongst Girard's personal effects. With this firm evidence
the military coup is averted, the Chiefs of Staff resign and Scott is defeated and
discredited.

COMMENT:
   Before *Seven Days in May* Lancaster had made a brief guest appearance in
John Huston's *The List of Adrian Messenger*, heavily disguised as a female
protester.
   Seven Days in May was filmed partly in Washington DC on a modest budget of
two million two hundred thousand dollars and President John F. Kennedy let it be
known that he thought the film was important and should be made. Released in
January 1964 the film was the number thirteen money-maker that year taking
three million four hundred thousand dollars.

   'As always Lancaster conveys power with the minimum of effort. He never lets
the military monster seem anything but a man of deep-seated, if misguided
integrity.'

Evening News

   'Burt Lancaster gives an excellent performance as the General, cool, sensible
and the absolute opposite of the raving dictator figure of convention.'

The Times

   'Burt Lancaster as the megalomaniac four-star general is mad with power,
crazy with patriotism, a crisp-talking Napoleon of the Atomic Age.'

Daily Express

THE TRAIN

(USA/France/Italy 1964)
RUNNING TIME: 140 minutes

Les Artistes Associés/Ariane/Dear Film

CAST: Burt Lancaster (Labiche), Paul Scofield (Von Waldheim), Jeanne Moreau (Christine), Suzanne Flon (Mlle. Villard), Michel Simon (Papa Boule), Wolfgang Preiss (Herren), Albert Remy (Didont), Charles Millot (Pesquet), Richard Munch (Von Lubitz), Jacques Marin (Jacques), Paul Bonifas (Spinet)

DIRECTOR: John Frankenheimer
PRODUCER: Jules Bricken
ASSOCIATE PRODUCER: Bernard Farrel
SCREENPLAY: Franklin Coen, Frank Davis and Walter Bernstein from the novel
          Le Front de l'Art by Rose Valland
PRODUCTION DESIGNER: Willy Holt
DIRECTOR OF PHOTOGRAPHY: Jean Tournier and Walter Wottiz
EDITOR: David Bretherton and Gabriel Rongier
SOUND: Joseph de Bretagne
PRODUCTION MANAGER: Robert Velin
MUSIC: Maurice Jarre
COSTUMES: Jean Zay

PLOT SYNOPSIS:
Paris, 2 August 1944. Colonel Von Waldheim of the Third Reich has been protecting irreplaceable French art treasures for over four years. In the face of the Allied advance Von Waldheim hurries to ship the paintings back to Germany. A museum curator, Villard, contacts the resistance to stop the loss of the national heritage. Railway inspector Labiche is unwilling to risk lives for art, more concerned with stopping an armaments train on his route.

Labiche's task is to delay the armaments train long enough to provide an open-air target for Allied bombers. He succeeds in this, but the obvious attempts to sabotage the arts train running on the same line, are discovered. Patriotic old engineer Papa Boule is arrested and shot. Von Waldheim orders Labiche to take personal responsibility for the train reaching Germany.

Labiche and his resistance colleagues perpetrate an elaborate hoax; the Germans are tricked into thinking the train is headed for the fatherland whilst Labiche has travelled in a circle and wrecks the engine in a spectacular crash. Reprisals are swift; many railway men and civilians are shot.

Labiche has been wounded and hides out in the cellar of a local hotel run by Christine. He is informed by the Resistance that the art treasures must be saved at all costs – the repaired carriages are to be painted white as a marker of safe passage to Allied bombers. Von Waldheim realises this and seizes it as a right of way to Germany. Labiche sabotages the track, derailing the train permanently. Von Waldheim attempts to use a passing convoy of trucks to convey the paintings but he is refused permission as all transport is required for the German retreat. Left alone with the treasures Von Waldheim is shot by Labiche who walks back to town. The treasures are left strewn across the countryside.

(Photo: Les Artistes Associés/Ariane/Dear Film)

COMMENT:

The Train began filming in Paris in August 1963 under the direction of Arthur Penn. However, after several days Penn left over 'artistic differences' and Lancaster asked Frankenheimer to fly over and make the film. The producer received the complete co-operation of the French railways who provided stations and obsolete rolling stock. The film used no models or process shots and several camera units were destroyed in capturing the crashes and explosions. Rain and heavy fogs caused delays in production and the film went over budget and was not completed until May 1964.

The only flaw in an otherwise convincing and persuasive thriller was the dubbing. Lancaster ruefully confided to Frankenheimer; 'My God, if only we had started this together, I would have played it with a French accent. Then we wouldn't have had to dub the other actors into that hoarse, American-English, and the entire film would have been more convincing.'

The film was number nineteen in the 1965 American box-office chart, taking three million four hundred and fifty thousand dollars.

'the acting is magnificent, Scofield is quite brilliant as the colonel, Lancaster has rarely done anything better than his Labiche.'

The Sun

'Scofield, prowling around like a caged puma, is magnificent. Lancaster makes the perfect human counterpart to him.'

Daily Express

THE HALLELUJAH TRAIL

(USA 1965)

RUNNING TIME: 167 minutes

Mirisch/Kappa Productions

CAST: Burt Lancaster (Col. Thadeus Gearhart), Lee Remick (Cora Massingale), Jim Hutton (Capt. Paul Slater), Pamela Tiffin (Louise Gearhart), Donald Pleasence (Oracle Jones), Brian Keith (Frank Wallingham), Martin Landau (Chief Walks-Stooped-Over), Tom Stern (Kevin O'Flaherty), Whit Bissell (Hobbs)

DIRECTOR: John Sturges
PRODUCER: John Sturges
ASSOCIATE PRODUCER: Robert E. Relyea
SCREENPLAY: John Gay from the novel by Bill Gulick
ART DIRECTOR: Cary Odell
DIRECTOR OF PHOTOGRAPHY: Robert Surtees
EDITOR: Ferris Webster
SOUND: Robert Martin
PRODUCTION MANAGER: Nate H. Edwards
MUSIC: Elmer Bernstein
COSTUMES: Edith Head

PLOT SYNOPSIS:

Colorado, 1867. Denver faces the onset of winter with only ten days supply of whisky left in the city. To combat this terrible state of affairs six hundred barrels of whisky are sent in forty wagons with a Cavalry escort as protection against possible Indian attacks.

Cora Templeton Massingale, a crusader against the evils of drink, is informed of the shipment by the teetotal editor of the local newspaper. She is determined to head off the whisky and demands the protection of the army which is reluctanly provided by Colonel Thadeus Gearhart and his B Troop. His daughter, Louise, is a fervent admirer of Miss Massingale but is also in love with Captain Paul Slater who heads A Troop in charge of the whisky shipment.

The plot thickens when two other groups join the whisky trail; a band of Indians and members of the Citizen's Militia from Denver. They all converge during a muddled battle in a sandstorm. Later Gearhart assumes overall command but the Indians refuse to leave the wagon train without acquiring the whisky. To prove their point they kidnap Cora's temperance women as hostages. Cora is a resourceful woman however, and utilises some explosively corked French champagne to see off the Indian threat. Totally bewildered by the events around him Gearhart can only marvel at her ingenuity. Cora manages to deposit all the whisky in quicksands, but two decidedly thirsty citizens bide their time waiting for the occasional barrel to rise to the surface.

(Photo: Mirisch/Kappa Productions)

COMMENT:

Based on a little known historical incident *The Hallelujah Trail* reunited Lancaster with the director of *Gunfight at the OK Corral* – John Sturges. Filming began in July 1964 with exteriors shot in Gallup, New Mexico and the interiors completed at Paramount and the Sam Goldwyn Studios.

The completed film originally ran nearly three hours and was designed to accommodate an intermission. First reactions to the film were disappointing and, after some editing and the loss of the intermission, *The Hallelujah Trail* went on general release.

'Mr Lancaster plays dead straight and Miss Remick archly flutters her eyelids to cover up her own deficiency in natural comedy talent. But both are always likeable if not very laughable.'

Daily Mail

'Lancaster, a commanding presence as always, looks permanently flabbergasted over his first venture into out-and-out farce.'

Time

'Burt Lancaster looks bored to death.'

Monthly Film Bulletin

THE PROFESSIONALS

(USA 1966)

RUNNING TIME: 117 minutes

Pax Enterprises

CAST: Burt Lancaster (Bill Dolworth), Lee Marvin (Henry Fardan), Robert Ryan (Hans Ehrengard), Woody Strode (Jacob Sharp), Claudia Cardinale (Maria Grant), Ralph Bellamy (J.W. Grant), Jack Palance (Capitan Raza), Marie Gomez (Chiquita), Joe de Santis (Ortega), Vaughn Taylor (Banker Stamp)

DIRECTOR: Richard Brooks
PRODUCER: Richard Brooks
SCREENPLAY: Richard Brooks from the novel *A Mule for the Marquesa* by Frank O'Rourke
ART DIRECTOR: Edward S. Haworth
DIRECTOR OF PHOTOGRAPHY: Conrad Hall
EDITOR: Peter Zinner
SOUND: Charles J.Rice, William Randall Jr. and Jack Haynes
PRODUCTION MANAGER: Lee Lukather
MUSIC: Maurice Jarre
COSTUMES: Jack Mastell

PLOT SYNOPSIS:
    1917. Wealthy rancher J.W. Grant hires four soldiers of fortune to cross the border into Mexico and recover his beautiful young wife Maria who has been abducted by Raza, a fierce bandit. Each of the four is a professional in his own field; Dolworth, an explosives expert; Fardan is accomplished in weaponry; Ehrengard a master horseman and Sharp, tracker extraordinary and a fine marksman with both bow and arrow and knife.
    The quartet make their way through desert and mountain land eventually coming upon Raza and his men. However, they learn that Maria is not a kidnap victim but has fled her cold, heartless husband to be with the man she loves –Raza. Dolworth is all for leaving the couple in peace but their leader, Fardan, insists that a contract is a contract and Maria has to be rescued. Using Dolworth's dynamite and Sharp's arrows they manage to secure Maria and head back to Grant. Raza and his men are hot on their heels and Maria attempts to escape at every opportunity. To give the others a head start Dolworth remains behind and dynamites a mountainside; a wounded Raza is the only survivor apart from Dolworth himself.
    The four return Maria to Grant along with their prisoner Raza, and thus their obligations are fulfilled. Grant is revealed in the villainous light painted by Maria all along and, effecting the escape of Maria and Raza, they all join forces and head for Mexico.

COMMENT:
The Professionals was Lee Marvin's first film after his Oscar-winning *Cat Ballou*. When first approached by his *Elmer Gantry* director Lancaster had assumed he was being offered the rôle of the leader of the mercenaries. Brooks felt

104

(Photo: Pax Enterprises)

Lancaster to be boring as a staunch leader of men, and thought him better cast as the hell-for-leather explosives expert.

The film was made on locations in Nevada, including the Valley of Fire State Park, Death Valley and the upper reaches of Lake Mead with Las Vegas close at hand. It was something of a return to his 'muscles and teeth' days for Lancaster who observed; 'The Professionals set out to be an entertaining, ribald kind of Western. There are still a bulk of people who like to go to a pure escapist film, and these films are bread and butter. The Professionals is a good film – highly entertaining. People were stimulated and excited by it.'

'The cast know what they are doing to an enviable degree of professionalism: Burt Lancaster (is) engagingly cynical as a rebel turned money-loving mercenary.'
The Sun

'Mr Lancaster is in especially good form: the athlete's beautiful movements and, giving edge to the whole film, the quality of genial, wolfish delight in battle, which is his peculiar contribution to the cinema of action.'
The Sunday Times

THE SWIMMER

(USA 1968)

RUNNING TIME: 94 minutes

Horizon/Dover Productions

CAST: Burt Lancaster (Ned Merrill), Janet Landgard (Julie Hooper), Janice Rule (Shirley Abbott), Tony Bickley (Donald Westerhazy), Marge Champion (Peggy Forsburgh), Nancy Cushman (Mrs Halloran), Bill Fiore (Howie Hunsacker), John Garfield Jr. (Ticket Seller), Kim Hunter (Betty Graham)

DIRECTORS: Frank Perry and Sydney Pollack
PRODUCERS: Frank Perry and Roger Lewis
SCREENPLAY: Eleanor Perry from the short story by John Cheever
ART DIRECTOR: Peter Dohanos
DIRECTOR OF PHOTOGRAPHY: David L. Quaid
EDITORS: Sidney Katz, Carl Lerner and Pat Somerset
SOUND: Willard Goodman
PRODUCTION MANAGER: Joseph Manduke
MUSIC: Marvin Hamlisch
COSTUMES: Anna Hill Johnstone

PLOT SYNOPSIS:

Connecticut. One summer Sunday Ned Merrill appears out of the blue at the swimming pool of some friends, dressed only in swimming trunks, and informs them of his intention to make his way home by swimming across county in his friends' pools. He is given a cheery greeting and obviously has not seen his friends for some time but he seems at home in this comfortable, middle-class milieu.

As his marathon swim progresses the façade of friendliness slips and he is received with growing embarrassment and unease. Julie Hooper, a former babysitter for the Merrill household, swims alongside him for part of the route but is shocked that a man of his age should try to make a pass at her. His friends begin to show open hostility at his presence – the Biswangers throw him out as a gatecrasher, the elderly Hallorans are surprised that he does not beg them for money and Shirly Abbot, once his mistress, bitterly resents his re-appearance in her life.

At the community swimming pool he is ridiculed and jeered at as a failure. As dusk falls and the rain pours he reaches his own home but the gate is rusted and the rooms gloomy and deserted; there is no sign of life. He falls to the ground, sobbing in despair.

COMMENT:

John Cheever's short story of middle-aged disillusionment and the sour underbelly of the American Dream had first appeared in the *New Yorker* magazine. In preparation for the rather unpromising screen material Lancaster underwent three months of swimming lessons to help him overcome mild hydrophobia.

The production was filmed in Connecticut's Fairfield County and was completed in 1966 although unreleased until two years later. Columbia Pictures

(Photo: Horizon/Dover Productions)

had little faith in the commercial value of the film and ordered certain sequences to be reshot. The original director, Frank Perry, protested and Sydney Pollack was hired to do the retakes. *The Swimmer* was a major failure at the box-office.

'It must be the most pretentious piece of symbolism ever to come out of Hollywood.'

The Sun

'Burt deserves a gold medal for his artistic high-dive.'

News of the World

107

THE SCALPHUNTERS

(USA 1968)

RUNNING TIME: 102 minutes

A Bristol/Norlan Production

CAST: Burt Lancaster (Joe Bass), Shelley Winters (Kate), Telly Savalas (Jim Howie), Ossie Davis (Joseph Winfield Lee), Armando Silvestre (Two Crows), Dabney Coleman (Jed), Paul Picerni (Frank), Dan Vadis (Yuma), Nick Cravat (Yancy)

DIRECTOR: Sydney Pollack
PRODUCERS: Jules Levy, Arthur Gardner and Arnold Laven
SCREENPLAY: William Norton
ART DIRECTOR: Frank Arrigo
DIRECTOR OF PHOTOGRAPHY: Duke Callaghan and Richard Moore
EDITOR: John Woodcock
SOUND: Jesus Gonzalez Gancy
PRODUCTION MANAGERS: Henry Spitz and Jack W. Corrick
MUSIC: Elmer Bernstein
COSTUMES: Joe Drury

PLOT SYNOPSIS:

Fur trapper Joe Bass is forced into trading his winter's pelts for the life of a well-educated black slave Joseph Lee. He agrees, aware that a slave will fetch a good price and persuaded by the barrel of a Kiowa Indian gun that the scheme is in his best interest. Bass intends to wait for the contents of a keg of rum to take effect on the Indians and then hijack the furs back. Bass and Lee strike up a wary friendship but before they can act the Indians are slaughtered by a gang of scalphunters. Only the chief, Two Crows, survives.

The scalphunters, led by Jim Howie and his cantankerous woman Kate, are now the proud owners of Bass's furs. When Lee inadvertently breaks from cover he too is added to Howie's haul. Lee ingratiates himself with Kate and is reluctant to help Bass when he learns that the scalphunters are destined for Mexico; in Mexico there are laws against slavery.

Bass makes several solo bids to recapture the furs, depleting Howie's numbers in the process. Eventually Howie sends Lee to bargain with Bass and a deal is struck. However, Howie double-crosses them, attacking and binding Bass. Lee intervenes and kills Howie, attempting to run off with the furs before Bass escapes from his bonds. The two fight to a standstill in a mammoth brawl. Two Crows and more Indians return taking Kate as a new squaw woman and Bass's furs.

Now working harmoniously with Bass, Lee reckons the two cases of whisky owned by Kate will have taken effect by nightfall and, together, they can retrieve the furs.

COMMENT:

Filming of this Western began on 23 February 1967 in Durango and Torreon in Mexico and provided a fitting screen culmination to Lancaster's involvement in the Civil Rights Movement throughout the 1960s.

(Photo: Bristol/Norlan Production)

During the lengthy shooting schedule Lancaster passed the time by learning Spanish and attending an operatic festival in Durango. On *The Scalphunters* he was surrounded by familiar faces, having worked with Telly Savalas, Nick Cravat and Shelley Winters on several occasions. Sydney Pollack had now established himself as a director with credits including the award-winning *Slender Thread* (1965) and *This Property is Condemned* (1966).

'As usual, Burt Lancaster brings a combination of star quality and talent to his rôle as the tough but human fur-trapper.'

The Sun

'Lancaster, naturally, dominates all including the landscape but, with this team, only a great star could do it.'

Sunday Express

CASTLE KEEP

(USA 1969)
RUNNING TIME: 106 minutes

Filmways Production

CAST: Burt Lancaster (Maj. Falconer), Patrick O'Neal (Capt. Beckham), Jean-Pierre Aumont (The Count), Peter Falk (Sgt. Rossi), Astrid Heeren (Thérèse), Scott Wilson (Capt. Clearboy), Tony Bill (Lt. Amberjack), Al Freeman Jr. (Pte. Benjamin), James Patterson (Elk), Bruce Dern (Billy Bix)

DIRECTOR: Sydney Pollack
PRODUCERS: Martin Ranshoff and John Calley
ASSOCIATE PRODUCERS: Edward L. Rissien
SCREENPLAY: Daniel Taradash and David Rayfiel from the novel by William Eastlake
PRODUCTION DESIGNER: Rino Mondellini
DIRECTOR OF PHOTOGRAPHY: Henri Decae
EDITOR: Malcolm Cooke
SOUND: Antoine Petitjean
PRODUCTION MANAGER: Ludmilla Goulian
MUSIC: Michael Legrand
COSTUMES: Jacques Fonteray

PLOT SYNOPSIS:
Winter, 1944. As the War in Europe draws to a close, one-eyed Major Falconer, his captain, a lieutenant and five enlisted men come upon a majestic tenth century castle in the Ardennes. The castle belongs to the Malderais family and the Count invites Falconer and his men to use it as their billet.

Falconer decides to use the castle as a military stronghold against the Germans despite its architectural importance and priceless art treasures. The wily count uses the situation to maximum advantage. He allows Falconer to make love to his wife, Thérèse, in the hope of producing the heir which he cannot sire whilst also enlisting the aid of the captain, an art historian, to prevent the castle's destruction. The other men amuse themselves in various ways, with the local brothel, The Red Queen, proving a hive of activity.

When the Germans arrive the men unite under Falconer's command and make a stand against the enemy. The Count is shot dead whilst trying to negotiate the safety of the Castle with the Germans. In a hard fought battle Falconer and his men are killed off one by one. The only survivors of the conflagration are Thérèse and a young black private who has been attempting to write a great novel about his experiences. Falconer had ordered him to escort Thérèse to safety. Once they are free of the Castle it begins to disintegrate.

COMMENT:
A rather incoherent film *Castle Keep* was a costly failure, filmed entirely on location in Yugoslavia. The beautiful castle seen in the film was constructed especially for the production and, together with the large number of extras and the vast quantities of blank ammunition, amounted to a hefty bill.

(Photo: Filmways Production)

Although Lancaster and Sydney Pollack had argued during the making of *The Scalphunters* they agreed to work together again. Lancaster later claimed; 'He was the man who really worked me the hardest, and the man I best communicated with.'

'It is always a little sad to find a picture that aims for the stars and ends up in the treetops . . . Indeed, the entire film, for all its elaborate production, falls between the stools of Mr Lancaster's heroics and its own anti-war intentions.'

Saturday Review

GYPSY MOTHS

(USA 1969)
RUNNING TIME: 110 minutes

Frankenheimer-Lewis Productions for MGM

CAST: Burt Lancaster (Mike Rettig), Deborah Kerr (Elizabeth Brandon), Gene Hackman (Joe Browdy), Scott Wilson (Malcolm Webson), William Windom (V. John Brandon), Bonnie Bedelia (Annie Burke), Sheree North (Waitress), Carl Reinde (Pilot), Ford Rainey (Stand Owner), John Napier (Dick Donford)

DIRECTOR: John Frankenheimer
PRODUCERS: Hal Landers and Bobby Roberts
EXECUTIVE PRODUCER: Edward Lewis
SCREENPLAY: William Hanley from the novel by James Drought
PRODUCTION DESIGNERS: George W. Davis and Cary Odell
DIRECTOR OF PHOTOGRAPHY: Philip Lathrop
EDITOR: Henry Berman
SOUND: Tom Overton
PRODUCTION MANAGER: Jim Henderling
MUSIC: Elmer Bernstein
COSTUMES: Bill Thomas

PLOT SYNOPSIS:
Three sky-divers, Rettig, Browdy and Webson, tour the small towns of the American mid-West performing death-defying stunts and feats of daring. On 2 July they arrive at Bridgeville in Kansas. It is the town in which Webson was raised as a boy and his uncle Professor Brandon and Aunt Elizabeth still live there. The divers are invited to spend a few days with the Brandons.

Rettig senses that the Brandon marriage has long gone cold and is attracted to Elizabeth. Uncharacteristically he agrees to lecture on sky-diving at a women's club meeting. In the evening the three divers go their separate ways; Browdy picks up a topless dancer, Webson dreams of college girl Annie and Rettig strolls the town with Elizabeth. When the two return to the house they make love, secretly observed by Brandon, but Elizabeth lacks the courage to leave when Rettig asks her to come away with him.

The climax of the following day's air show is the dangerous 'cape stunt' performed by Rettig. He deliberately doesn't pull his 'chute and falls to his death.

Webson and Browdy arrange a special Fourth of July memorial show which will consist of one jump, the same 'cape stunt', this time performed by Webson. On the evening prior to the show Webson and Annie make love. On the next day Webson lands safely but claims it will be his last jump and leaves Bridgeville. Browdy heads for Hollywood, seeking to become a stuntman and the Brandons return to their old, orderly way of life.

COMMENT:
The Gypsy Moths was another attempt by Lancaster to explore a character for whom the dreams and ideals have faded. His last film to date with John Frankenheimer, it was another box-office failure.

112

(Photo: Frankenheimer – Lewis Productions)

Filmed in and around Wichita, Kansas during the summer of 1968 Lancaster later admitted that the film could have appeared pretentious.

'As he has grown older, Mr Lancaster has developed a capacity, unique in established stars, to 'give away' scenes that his status in the movie pecking order entitles him to dominate. He did it in *Castle Keep*, he does it in *The Gypsy Moths* and he deserves full credit for his shrewd selflessness.'

Life

'The impact of the exotic when it affects conventional lives is always interesting. Mr Lancaster and Miss Kerr make it especially so.'

Evening News

AIRPORT

(USA 1969)
RUNNING TIME: 137 minutes

Ross Hunter Productions for Universal

CAST: Burt Lancaster (Mel Bakersfield), Dean Martin (Vernon Demarest), Jean
Seberg (Tanya Livingston), Jacqueline Bissett (Gwen Meighen), George
Kennedy (Joe Patroni), Helen Hayes (Ada Quonsett), Van Heflin (D.O.
Guerrero), Maureen Stapleton (Inez Guerrero), Barry Nelson (Anson Harris),
Lloyd Nolan (Harry Standish), Dana Wynter (Cindy Bakersfield), Barbara
Hale (Sarah Demarest)

DIRECTOR: George Seaton
PRODUCER: Ross Hunter
ASSOCIATE PRODUCER: Jacque Mapes
SCREENPLAY: George Seaton from the novel by Arthur Hailey
ART DIRECTORS: Alexander Golitzen and F. Preston Ames
DIRECTOR OF PHOTOGRAPHY: Ernest Laszlo
EDITOR: Stuart Gilmore
SOUND: Waldon O. Warson, David H. Moriarty and Ronald Pierce
PRODUCTION MANAGER: Raymond Gosnell
MUSIC: Alfred Newman
COSTUMES: Edith Head

PLOT SYNOPSIS:
    Lincoln Airport is at a crisis point facing the worst snow storms in six years.
Airport manager Mel Bakersfield attempts to keep the runways open aided by
maintenance engineer Joe Patroni and the sympathetic Tanya Livingston, a
passenger relations officer with Trans Global Airlines. He must combat local
residents threatening a $10 million damages suit, allegations of inefficiency from
his brother-in-law Vernon Demarest, and domestic pressures from his wife who
wants a divorce. When an incoming 'plane stops short, blocking runway 29,
Bakersfield cancels all engagements and swings into action.
    Demarest is the inspection pilot on Golden Argosy Flight 2 to Rome. On board
are his pregnant girlfriend, stewardess Gwen Meighen, and a passenger list that
includes veteran stowaway Ada Quonsett and D.O. Guerrero. Guerrero has
insured his life for $225,000 and plans to atone for past failures as a husband and
father by detonating an attaché case of dynamite in mid-air. His wife Inez
discovers that his flight is bound for Rome and not Milwaukee as she believed, the
authorities are alerted, and the flight ordered to return to Lincoln. On board
Demarest attempts to reason with Guerrero but in the ensuing panic the bomb
explodes blasting a hole in the side of the 'plane, killing Guerrero and severely
injuring Gwen.
    The stricken airliner heads for snowbound Lincoln where, against impossible
odds, Bakersfield and Patroni clear the blocked runway and the 'plane lands in
safety with all hands saved. The crisis averted, Bakersfield leaves for his first
breakfast with Tanya.

114

(Photo: Ross Hunter Productions)

COMMENT:

Filmed mainly at St Paul Airport in Minneapolis, *Airport* is unquestionably the most financially successful production with which Lancaster has ever been associated. The six million pound film version of Arthur Hailey's popular bestseller was the number one American film release in 1970 eventually realising more than forty-five million dollars and establishing itself as one of the most lucrative films of all time.

Helen Hayes won the Academy Award as Best Supporting Actress and thus became the first actress in the Academy's history to win both a major and a supporting Oscar.

Lancaster thought the film; 'the biggest piece of junk ever made' and the critics tended to agree. The success spawned three sequels – *Airport 1975*, *Airport '77* and *Airport '79-the Concorde*.

'*Airport* is bland, pre-digested entertainment of the old school; every stereotyped action is followed by a stereotyped reaction; clichés commenting on clichés.'

New Yorker

'The film is half over before we get to the bomb. But under George Seaton's direction Van Heflin's haunted terror, Maureen Stapleton's demented panic as the wife who tries too late to keep him off the plane and Burt Lancaster's brisk ground-to-air authority help to atone for the delay.'

Daily Mail

VALDEZ IS COMING

(USA 1970)
RUNNING TIME: 90 minutes

Norlan Productions

CAST: Burt Lancaster (Bob Valdez), Susan Clark (Gay Erin), Jon Cypher (Frank Tanner), Richard Jordan (R.L. Davis), Barton Heyman (El Segundo), Frank Silvera (Diego), Hector Elizondo (Mexican Rider), Phil Brown (Malson), Ralph Brown (Beaudry)

DIRECTOR: Edwin Sherin
PRODUCER: Ira Steiner
ASSOCIATE PRODUCER: Sam Manners
SCREENPLAY: Ronald Kibbee and David Rayfiel
ART DIRECTOR: Jose Maria Tapiador
DIRECTOR OF PHOTOGRAPHY: Gabor Pogany
EDITOR: James T. Heckart and George Rohrs
SOUND: H. Bud Alper
PRODUCTION MANAGER: Sam Manners
MUSIC: Charles Gross
COSTUMES: Lewis Brown

PLOT SYNOPSIS:
Local big-shot Frank Tanner lays siege to an out-of-the-way house believing the occupant, a reformed negro deserter, to have killed his mistress's husband. Many believe Tanner himself killed Gay Erin's husband and he is eager to clear his name. Councillor Bob Valdez, an ageing, paunchy Mexican, intervenes and, through the irresponsible action of Tanner's men, has to kill the negro. Learning of the latter's innocence Valdez is filled with remorse and attempts to take up a collection for the negro's widow woman. Local townsmen promise Valdez $100 if their money is matched by Tanner's. Valdez visits the Tanner ranch twice, on both occasions he is ridiculed and manhandled. On the second visit he is sent back to town tied to a heavy, wooden cross.
Dressed in his old cavalry uniform Valdez sets out to avenge his humiliation, sending the message 'Valdez is Coming'. Gaining access to Tanner's bedroom Valdez demands the $100 as a point of principle. When detected he escapes using Gay as a shield against Tanner's gunmen and heads for the mountains. In hiding Gay admits she killed her own husband and could have prevented the death of the negro. Evading capture Valdez kills eleven men before ultimately being taken at gunpoint, with Gay, to confront Tanner. At the showdown Tanner is left by his men to settle the score on his own, he will not fight Valdez and the matter ends there.

COMMENT:
Valdez is Coming followed on the trail of many contemporary American Westerns filmed in Spain. Outdoor locations were in Almeira and Credos with studio shooting at the Estudios Roma in Madrid. The company faced severe

(Photo: Norlan Production)

flooding in Almeira but, despite this setback, managed to finish three days ahead of schedule and under budget.

Valdez is Coming performed rather poorly at the box-office and it was now believed that Lancaster was accepting a smaller initial fee for any film appearances and adapting to changed times.

'Lancaster's brand of gritty honesty invests the film with a superiority which the script often tends to devaluate.'

Daily Mirror

'The luck of Valdez though, is in having Burt Lancaster to play him: an actor whose self-contained neatness of style belies the flamboyance of his appearance. He belongs to a dying breed; a real star.'

Sunday Telegraph

LAWMAN

(USA 1970)
RUNNING TIME: 99 minutes

Scimitar Productions

CAST: Burt Lancaster (Jered Maddox), Robert Ryan (Cotton Ryan), Lee J. Cobb (Vincent Bronson), Sheree North (Laura Shelby), Joseph Wiseman (Lucas), Robert Duvall (Vernon Adams), Albert Salmi (Harvey Stenbaugh), J.D. Cannon (Hurd Price), John McGiver (Mayor Sam Bolden)

DIRECTOR: Michael Winner
PRODUCER: Michael Winner
SCREENPLAY: Gerald Wilson
PRODUCTION DESIGNER: Stan Jolley
DIRECTOR OF PHOTOGRAPHY: Bob Paynter
EDITOR: Freddie Wilson
SOUND: Hugh Strain and Manuel Topete Blake
PRODUCTION MANAGERS: Clifton Brandon, Alberto Ferrer and Carlos Terron
MUSIC: Jerry Fielding
COSTUMES: Ron Beck

PLOT SYNOPSIS:
Letting off steam in the small town of Bannock, cattle-baron Vincent Bronson and his men accidentally kill an old man. Local lawman Jered Maddox is out of town but, on his return, he heads for Bronson's home ground of Sabbath to arrest the guilty men and bring them to trial.

The town of Sabbath feels beholden to Bronson and resents Maddox's presence, the marshall, Cotton Ryan, is in the pay of Bronson and will not act to help. When Bronson learns of the killing he attempts to make amends, offering to recompense the widow and pay off Maddox. Maddox refuses the offer and is resolute that the men will stand trial.

One of Bronson's men, Stenbaugh, confronts Maddox but is outgunned and dies. The townsfolk form a vigilante committee but lack the courage to drive Maddox out of town. An attempt to shoot him in the back fails and the man is arrested. Maddox leaves town in search of the remainder of Bronson's party. On the way he wounds and arrests Vernon Adams. The two rest for the night at Laura Shelby's ranch. Laura is an old flame of Maddox and she makes him question his rigid morality.

Riding back to Sabbath Maddox is determined to leave town and thereby end the senseless violence. However, Bronson's men demand revenge and conflict is inevitable. Maddox kills three men, including Bronson's son and Bronson is so grief-stricken that he commits suicide. Maddox leaves town, his task completed.

COMMENT:
Michael Winner's one and a half million pound Western filmed on a ten week schedule in Chupaderos, a village outside Durango in Mexico, *Lawman* received a great deal of publicity as the first Western made by an Englishman.

(Photo: Scimitar Productions)

The ebullient Winner is renowned for not shooting in a studio and for his speedy efficiency; Lancaster was impressed and stated; 'I find him engaging and buoyant and very intelligent, he keeps his set a lot of fun.'

'Mr Winner has wrung from Western old hands such as Mr Lancaster, Lee J. Cobb and Robert Ryan performances that convince without cliché.'
Sunday Telegraph

'Burt Lancaster, granite-faced and seemingly granite-hearted, is enough to give the most dedicated baddie the shivers when he rides into town.'
Daily Sketch

ULZANA'S RAID

(USA 1972)

RUNNING TIME: 103 minutes

A Carter DeHaven-Robert Aldrich Production

CAST: Burt Lancaster (McIntosh), Bruce Davison (Lt. Garnett DeBuin), Jorge Luke (Ke-Ni-Tay), Richard Jaeckel (Sergeant), Joaquin Martinez (Ulzana), Lloyd Bochner (Capt. Gates), Karl Swenson (Rikeyser), Douglass Watson (Major Cartwright), Dran Hamilton (Mrs Riordan), Nick Cravat (Trooper)

DIRECTOR: Robert Aldrich
PRODUCER: Carter DeHaven
ASSOCIATE PRODUCER: Alan Sharp
SCREENPLAY: Alan Sharp
ART DIRECTOR: James Vance
DIRECTOR OF PHOTOGRAPHY: Joseph Biroc
EDITOR: Michael Luciano
SOUND: Waldon O. Watson and Jim Alexander
PRODUCTION MANAGER: Ernest B. Wehmeyer
MUSIC: Frank de Vol

PLOT SYNOPSIS:
Led by their chief Ulzana a small group of Apache tribesmen escape from the San Carlos Indian Reservation. The cavalry at the nearby Fort Lowell play the incident down deciding to send a youthful officer into the field with a troop of men and instructions to track down the renegades. The inexperienced Lieutenant De Buin is aided by veteran Indian scout McIntosh and Ke-Ni-Tay, an Indian himself.

The Indians rampage, causing the brutal deaths of two army scouts and a homesteading couple. De Buin's Christian beliefs are appalled by the savagery but Ke-Ni-Tay explains the Apache code of gaining power through the death of one's enemies. Ulzana avoids a direct confrontation, deploying guerrilla tactics whilst DeBuin doggedly follows the trail. McIntosh discovers an Indian plan to turn back on the cavalry and massacre them, and attempts to turn the tables. Riding alone McIntosh succeeds in dispersing Ulzana's horses, killing one Indian and injuring another. The lieutenant reckons that Ulzana must seek fresh horses but arrives too late at the nearest homestead to save the lives of the inhabitants. One woman survives, she has been spared to force the lieutenant to split his force in escorting her to the safety of the fort. McIntosh realises this and decides to use the bait for the cavalry's own assault.

As expected, the Indians attack McIntosh's party, killing all save McIntosh and the woman. De Buin arrives to round up the renegades whilst Ke-Ni-Tay kills Ulzana with dignity. Badly injured McIntosh chooses to await death in the desert rather than ride back to Fort Lowell.

(Photo: Carter DeHaven – Robert Aldrich Production) Jorge Luke

COMMENT:

Lancaster's third Western in a row, *Ulzana's Raid* was begun after his stage work in the musical *Knickerbocker Holiday* where he had been coached by Frank Sinatra.

Filmed in Nogales, Arizona and Nevada, Lancaster reflected that; 'The man I played in *Ulzana's Raid* was a man who reflected my own feelings about life.'

Again the film did not fare too well at the box-office although the critical consensus seemed to be that the film contained one of the older Lancaster's best performances.

'A nice, solid characterisation by Burt Lancaster.'

Financial Times

'To their credit young Bruce Davison, Richard Jaeckel and Jorge Luke stand up sturdily to the matchless authority of Burt Lancaster.'

Sunday Telegraph

SCORPIO

(USA 1972)

RUNNING TIME: 114 minutes

Scimitar Productions for the Mirisch Corporation

CAST: Burt Lancaster (Cross), Alain Delon (Laurier), Paul Scofield (Zharkov), John Colicos (McLeod), Gayle Hunnicutt (Susan), J.D. Cannon (Filchock), Joanne Linville (Sarah), Melvin Stewart (Pick), Vladek Sheybal (Zemetkin), Mary Maude (Anne)

DIRECTOR: Michael Winner
PRODUCER: Walter Mirisch
SCREENPLAY: David W. Rintels and Gerald Wilson from a story by Rintels
ART DIRECTOR: Herbert Westbrook
DIRECTOR OF PHOTOGRAPHY: Robert Paynter
EDITOR: Freddie Wilson
SOUND: Brian Marshall
PRODUCTION MANAGERS: James Crawford, Laci Von Ronay and David Silver
MUSIC: Jerry Fielding
COSTUMES: Philippe Pickford

PLOT SYNOPSIS:
CIA chief, McLeod, believes that veteran operator Cross is a double agent and hires freelance killer Laurier to execute him whilst on a mission in Paris. Laurier, a pupil and admirer of Cross, does not fulfil his contract, doubting the validity of McLeod's suspicions. McLeod attempts to blackmail Laurier but eventually the men agree terms – 25,000 dollars plus Cross's job in Beirut in return for the latter's death.

Cross has gone into hiding in Vienna at the house of Zharkov, a retired Russian spy. Both men have grown tired and disillusioned with the spying game and Zharkov agrees to shelter Cross until his wife Sarah can join him from America. In America McLeod's callous hirelings accidentally kill Sarah; a much-disguised Cross returns to Washington and avenges her death by executing McLeod.

Meanwhile, Laurier, always convinced of Cross's innocence, has traced him to Vienna but decides to let the matter rest and return to Paris with his girlfriend Susan.

The CIA continue to pressurise Laurier into believing that Cross is defecting. When the CIA screen incriminating film Laurier is finally convinced and shocked to find that Susan has acted as Cross's clandestine courier. He kills Susan and Cross but is shot dead himself by the CIA who attempt to tie up all the loose ends.

COMMENT:
Lancaster's long-standing relationship with United Artists was coming to a close. He had enjoyed the right to refuse two scripts from every three offered and had recently rejected a Michael Winner project, *The Mechanic*, which was filmed with Charles Bronson. Keen to renew his association with Winner he accepted *Scorpio* despite a poor script.

(Photo: Scimitar Productions)

The title derived from the shared birth sign of Lancaster, Winner and Alain Delon. Locations included Paris, Vienna and Washington DC. On the last day of filming in Washington Lancaster presented the Chief of Police with a cheque for two thousand dollars in aid of the Police Boys' Club and as a thankyou for police co-operation during the filming.

Lancaster and Winner discussed working on *Death Wish* although studio executives considered Charles Bronson better box-office. Winner also sought him for a cameo in *Won, Ton, Ton* which never came to pass.

'(Lancaster) a far better actor than he is given credit for, he has worn well.'
The Sunday Times
'Cross is given the honest, upright, lantern-jawed treatment by Burt Lancaster.'
Spectator

EXECUTIVE ACTION

(USA 1973)

RUNNING TIME: 91 minutes

Wakefield Orloff

CAST: Burt Lancaster (Farrington), Robert Ryan (Foster), Will Geer (Ferguson), Gilbert Green (Paulitz), John Anderson (Halliday), Paul Carr (Chris), Colby Chester (Tim), Ed Lauter (Operations Chief), Richard Bull (Gunman), Lee Delano (Gunman), Walter Brooke (Smythe), Lloyd Gough (McCadden)

DIRECTOR: David Miller
PRODUCER: Edward Lewis
CO-PRODUCERS: Dan Bessie and Gary Horowitz
SCREENPLAY: Dalton Trumbo from a story by Mark Lane and Donald Freed
ART DIRECTOR: Kirk Axtell
DIRECTOR OF PHOTOGRAPHY: Robert Steadman
EDITORS: George Grenville and Irving Lerner
SOUND: Bruce Bisenz, Kirk Francis and Jock Putnam
PRODUCTION CO-ORDINATORS: Severo Perez and Frank Glenn
MUSIC: Randy Edelman
COSTUMES: Gerry Puhara

PLOT SYNOPSIS:
1963. A small group of powerful right-wing Americans, influential in business and government, begin planning the assassination of President John F. Kennedy. Convinced that Kennedy's liberal policies of seeking a rapprochement with the Russians and encouraging the Civil Rights movement are fundamentally opposed to their interests and, fearful of a Kennedy dynasty, they decide that his death is in the best interest of the country.

Farrington, the operations director, begins training a team of crack marksmen and sets the date for the assassination – 22 November, outside the Texas Book Depository in Dallas. Lee Harvey Oswald, a man who has defected to Russia and returned to the States, is selected as an appropriate scapegoat. A double implicates the real Oswald.

On 22 November shots ring out from a building, a grassy knoll and the Book Depository and the President is slain. The hired assassins escape into the crowd and Oswald is subsequently arrested for murder. He never stands trial; he is gunned down by nightclub owner Jack Ruby who has also been in on the conspiracy.

Foster, Ferguson and the other conspirators meet to celebrate their achievement – the end of the Kennedy régime. Their cheer is dampened by the unexpected news that Farrington has died of a heart attack. In the next three years eighteen of the material witnesses to the slaying all die.

COMMENT:
Executive Action was a project to which liberal Lancaster and the other actors were particularly committed. Everyone on the film worked for Equity minimum. At the time he explained; 'After a good deal of private research I was convinced

Robert Ryan *(Photo: Wakefield Orloff)*

there had been a conspiracy and the possibility that Oswald had been set up as a Communist fall-guy. Everything we say in *Executive Action* is based on evidence. If I had not been certain this was the case I would not have made the film. I was a Kennedy man. I knew there would be an outcry in some quarters, but I've never worried about what the public thinks. The only thing I took into consideration was the validity of the script.'

'Mr Lancaster, as always solidly persuasive, plays the man in charge of the assassination plan.'

The Sunday Times

'The operation is masterminded by Burt Lancaster, an impressive (though totally implausible) super hatchet-man.'

Evening News

THE MIDNIGHT MAN

(USA 1974)

RUNNING TIME: 117 minutes

Norlan Productions for Universal release

CAST: Burt Lancaster (Jim), Susan Clark (Linda), Cameron Mitchell (Quartz), Morgan Woodward (Clayborn), Harris Yulin (Casey), Robert Quarry (Dr Pritchet), Joan Lorring (Judy), Lawrence Dobkin (Mason), Ed Lauter (Leroy), Mills Watson (Cash), Charles Tyner (Ewing), Catherine Bach (Natalie), William Lancaster (King)

DIRECTOR: Roland Kibbee and Burt Lancaster
PRODUCERS: Roland Kibbee and Burt Lancaster
SCREENPLAY: Roland Kibbee and Burt Lancaster from the novel *The Midnight Lady and the Mourning Man* by David Anthony
PRODUCTION DESIGNER: James D. Vance
DIRECTOR OF PHOTOGRAPHY: Jack Priestley
EDITOR: Frank Morriss
SOUND: Melvin M. Metcalfe Snr.
PRODUCTION MANAGER: Donald Gold
MUSIC: Dave Grusin

PLOT SYNOPSIS:

South Carolina. Jim Slade, a former cop who has served time for killing his wife's lover, begins work as a security guard on a college campus. The job, from his old friend Quartz Willinger, is his new start in life.

One evening he discovers a break-in at the psychology lab; three tapes are missing on which students record their personal problems. Disdainful of the local law's capabilities, Slade begins his own investigations. He believes the thief sought recordings made by Natalie Clayborne and, when she is murdered, his suspicions are confirmed.

Following a number of leads Slade begins to unravel the mystery but he is warned by his friend Quartz and his parole officer and lover Linda, not to become involved. Senator Clayborne, Natalie's father, attempts to hire Slade to find the crucial tape. Slade is attacked by three hoodlums and later, Swanson, Clayborne's secretary, is murdered in mistake for Slade. Clayborne confesses that the tape details his incestuous relationship with his daughter, and a student, King, deduces the meaning of a poetic clue. King is killed and Slade arrested for the murder, although released on bail. He pieces together the mystery, reporting his findings to Sheriff Casey. Linda, who was also Natalie's parole officer and lover, had been involved in an elaborate blackmailing plot with nightclub owner Eddie Lamarr and Quartz. When Natalie had refused to join their scheme she had been murdered, thus triggering the train of events which Slade has uncovered. To Slade's disgust Linda had planned to share the money with him and escape together.

(Photo: Norlan Productions) Nick Cravat

COMMENT:

Lancaster was drawn into his various functions on *The Midnight Man* by his long-time associate Ronald Kibbee. Kibbee explained; 'The *Midnight Man* was a concession to me because I wanted to make some money. It certainly wasn't the kind of project Burt would have picked for himself, and unfortunately it hasn't so far worked out to be very profitable. Burt is one of the most intellectual actors I've ever known. He has no taste for pulp fiction and I had to talk him into reading *The Midnight Lady and the Mourning Man*, which is pulp. Lancaster is the most uncompromising star I know of.'

Filming from February 1973 in South Carolina locations *The Midnight Man* was not a success and received only a minimal exposure in British cinemas.

'Nine out of ten to Burt Lancaster for not only starring but helping to write, produce and direct such a complicated and irrational structure.'

Morning Star

'Burt Lancaster (is) turning into an attractive, hard-working actor as superstardom fades.'

Time

127

THE CONVERSATION PIECE

(Italy/France 1974)
RUNNING TIME: 119 minutes

A Co-Production of Rusconi Film (Rome) and
Gaumont International SARL (Paris)

CAST: Burt Lancaster (The Professor), Helmut Berger (Konrad), Silvana Mangano (Countess Bianca Brumonti), Claudia Marsani (Lietta), Stefano Patrizi (Stefano), Elvira Cortese (Erminia), Dominique Sanda (The Professor's Mother), Claudia Cardinale (The Professor's Wife)

DIRECTOR: Luchino Visconti
PRODUCER: Giovanni Bertolucci
SCREENPLAY: Luchino Visconti, Suso Cecchi D'Amico and Enrico Medioli
ART DIRECTOR: Mario Garbuglia
DIRECTOR OF PHOTOGRAPHY: Pasqualino de Santis
EDITOR: Ruggero Mastroianni
SOUND: Claudio Maielli
PRODUCTION MANAGER: Lucio Trentini
MUSIC: Franco Mannino
COSTUMES: Vera Marzot
ORIGINAL LANGUAGE TITLE: Gruppo di Famiglia in un Inferno

PLOT SYNOPSIS:
Rome. The Professor, an ageing recluse, lives alone in his grand house surrounded by an impressive collection of eighteenth century family groups or 'conversation pieces'. Countess Bianca Brumonti invades his orderly existence and persuades him to rent his top-floor flat to her daughter Lietta and boyfriend Stefano. The Countess's German gigolo Konrad also occupies the flat and the family sets about redesigning the building.

The Professor regards Konrad with open hostility, viewing him as loud, offensive and vulgar. However, a chance encounter reveals a mutual appreciation of Mozart and a common love of art. One evening the Professor hears the noise of a fight and finds that Konrad has been attacked. The Professor tends him and a relationship develops between the two.

In gregarious mood the Professor invites his new-found family to dinner. A heated debate arises between the right-wing Stefano and the left-wing Konrad who determines to leave the Countess. The Professor attempts to convey how his life has been opened up and his horizons broadened by their stay at his house. Later that evening there is an explosion on the top floor and Konrad is found dead, probably murdered for his anti-Fascist activities. The Professor is distraught and suffers a coronary thrombosis from which he may, or may not, recover.

COMMENT:
At a time when Lancaster was far from excited by much of the material offered him a reunion with Visconti must have appeared to hold promise. Laurence Olivier had been the first choice for the rôle of the Professor with Audrey Hepburn as the Countess.

(Photo: Rusconi Film and Gaumont International)

The Conversation Piece was Visconti's return to film-making after a two year absence through illness; he directed much of the apparently autobiographical work from his wheelchair in Rome. The film was a success in Europe but a disaster in the English-speaking market. At the film's American première at the New York Film Festival *The Conversation Piece* was booed and jeered by the audience.

'Lancaster alone lends the film some of the dignity and resonance it must have had in Visconti's head.'

Financial Times

'It has two resonant performances by Mr Lancaster and Miss Mangano which complement each other marvellously.'

Sunday Telegraph

MOSES

(Italy/United Kingdom 1975)
RUNNING TIME: 141 minutes

RAI (Rome)/ITC (London)

CAST: Burt Lancaster (Moses), William Lancaster (Moses as a young man), Anthony Quayle (Aaron), Irene Papas (Zipporah), Ingrid Thulin (Miriam), Laurent Tiezieff (Pharaoh), Yousef Shiloah (Dathan), Aharon Ipale (Joshua), Marina Berti (Eliseba), Melba Englander (Pharaoh's Wife), Richard Johnson (Narrator)

DIRECTOR: Gianfranco De Bosio
PRODUCER: Vicenzo Labella
SCREENPLAY: Anthony Burgess, Vittorio Bonicelli and Gianfranco De Bosio
ART DIRECTOR: Pierluigi Basile
DIRECTOR OF PHOTOGRAPHY: Marcello Gatti
EDITORS: Gerry Hambling, Peter Boita, John Guthridge, Alberto Gallitti and
        Freddie Wilson
SOUND: Win Ryder
PRODUCTION MANAGER: Bernard J. Kingham
MUSIC: Ennio Morricone
COSTUMES: Enrico Sabbatini

PLOT SYNOPSIS:
    In an attempt to decimate the tribes of Israel, the Egyptian Pharaoh orders the execution of every male Hebrew child. Moses birth goes undetected and he is set adrift in a wicker basket. Pharaoh's daughter discovers him floating on the Nile and raises him as an Egyptian.
    Enraged by the actions of a cruel overseer Moses kills him and escapes to the wilderness where he meets and marries Zipporah. From a burning bush he is commanded by God to lead the people of Israel to the Promised Land of Canaan. Moses attempts to persuade Pharaoh to let the Israelites go but the latter is adamant in his refusal. Moses invokes many plagues from frogs to locusts to the Angel of Death before Pharaoh succumbs to his entreaties. Accompanied by his brother, Aaron, Moses leads the people of Israel on their long journey; parting the Red Sea to speed their travel and engulfing the Egyptian cavalry in the reconstituted waters.
    Later Moses climbs Mount Sinai to receive the Ten Commandments. Whilst he is gone the people grow restless, worship false Gods and sacrifice a young girl. When Moses returns he destroys the tablets in anger and avenges the sacrileges perpetrated. Returning to the mountain he learns of the Israelites punishment — to wander in the wilderness for forty years. Moses himself is forbidden to enter the Promised Land. Eventually the Ark of the Covenant is built to house the new tablets and the Israelites are free to claim their inheritance. Moses is given a vision of the Promised Land before he dies.

(Photo: RAI/ITC)

COMMENT:

Strictly speaking *Moses* was a television series and marked Lancaster's first major appearance in that medium. Although reluctant to accept the part Lancaster was persuaded by international impressario Lew Grade into spending the necessary twelve months on locations in Israel and Italy.

Moses; the Lawgiver was seen as a weekly sixty minute show on CBS television in America before being edited down into a feature film for Europe. Lancaster's son William, who had appeared in his father's *Midnight Man*, here plays the young Moses.

Attending a London première in 1976 Lancaster claimed; 'I do not derive any comfort from orthodox religion. Life is simply to be lived within the limits of your knowledge and within the concept of what you would like to see yourself be.'

'If Moses supposes the show is all roses, then Moses supposes erroneously.'
Films Illustrated

1900

(Italy/France/Germany 1975)
RUNNING TIME: 248 minutes

PEA (Rome)/Artistes Associés (Paris)/Artemis (West Berlin)

CAST: Robert De Niro (Alfredo), Gerard Depardieu (Olmo Dalco), Dominique Sanda (Ada Fiastri Paulham), Donald Sutherland (Attila), Burt Lancaster (Alfredo Berlinghieri), Sterling Haydn (Leo Dalco), Stefania Sandrelli (Anita Foschi), Laura Betti (Regina), Alida Valli (Signora Pioppi)

DIRECTOR: Bernardo Bertolucci
PRODUCER: Alberto Grimaldi
SCREENPLAY: Bernardo Bertolucci, Franco Arcalli and Giuseppe Bertolucci
ART DIRECTOR: Ezio Frigerio
DIRECTOR OF PHOTOGRAPHY: Vittorio Storaro
EDITOR: Franco Arcalli
SOUND: Claudio Maielli
PRODUCTION MANAGER: Mario Di Blase
MUSIC: Ennio Morricone
COSTUMES: Gitt Magrini
ORIGINAL LANGUAGE TITLE: Novocento

PLOT SYNOPSIS:
The province of Emilia, Italy. During the summer of 1900 two boys are born on the same day on the Berlinghieri estate; Alfredo is the grandson of grand old patriarch Alfredo and Olmo is born into the large family of estate worker Leo Dalco. The two boys grow up and share their childhood. Alfredo has great hopes for his grandson. Despairing of his eldest son, Ottavio, who has left the estate for the lure of the city, Alfredo passes on the management of his land to his ineffectual younger son Giovanni and wife Eleanora before hanging himself.

Giovanni attempts to modernise the estate; evicting the poor tenants and surviving a disastrous storm. The peasants begin to mobilise in opposition and Leo Dalco dies quietly in the fields.

During the First World War Alfredo remains at home whilst the estate dwindles under the vicious manager Attila. Olmo is drafted into the army, returning to join with schoolteacher Anita in the struggle against fascism. Olmo and Anita marry but the latter dies during childbirth. Following his father's death Alfredo marries the sophisticated Ada Fiastra Paulham but their marriage is unsuccessful and she finds solace in heavy drinking.

Attila profits from the rise of Mussolini and is ruthless in his persecution of the peasants. However, when the wheel turns and Mussolini falls from power the peasants exact their revenge against the ruling classes. Alfredo's life is saved by the intervention of Olmo. In old age the two revert to their close friendship, strengthened since boyhood.

(Photo: PEA/Artistes Associés/Artemis)

COMMENT:

Following the international success of Bertolucci's *Last Tango in Paris* the young Italian director was able to set up a deal to finance his epic history of the twentieth century. Filming over a period of eleven months the cameras began rolling in July 1974 on a budget which eventually bloated to some nine million dollars. The main base for the film was Bertolucci's birthplace of the University city of Parma.

The Italian entry at the Cannes Film Festival of 1976, the original running time was some five and a half hours, which was something of a problem as Bertolucci's deal with Paramount stipulated the delivery of a three hours fifteen minutes film. In Britain the edited *1900* was released in two parts.

Lancaster was among the first to complete work on the film in a rôle originally intended for Orson Welles.

'Burt Lancaster brings a tired dignity to the padrone who cannot accept sexless old age or his weakling progeny.'

What's On in London

'Splendidly acted by all concerned, the first half of the epic has warmth and a genuine feeling of rough humanity about it.'

Daily Express

'One of the most unsatisfactory and disappointing epics I've ever looked forward to seeing.'

The Guardian

BUFFALO BILL AND THE INDIANS

(USA 1976)

RUNNING TIME: 123 minutes

Dino De Laurentiis Productions

CAST: Paul Newman (Buffalo Bill), Joel Gray (Nate Salsbury), Kevin McCarthy (Maj. John Burke), Allan Nichols (Col. Prentiss Ingraham), Harvey Keitel (Ed Goodman), Mike Kaplan (Jules Keen), Bert Remsen (Crutch), Burt Lancaster (Ned Buntline), Geraldine Chaplin (Annie Oakley), Will Sampson (Interpreter), Shelley Duvall (Mrs Cleveland)

DIRECTOR: Robert Altman
PRODUCER: Robert Altman
EXECUTIVE PRODUCER: David Susskind
SCREENPLAY: Alan Rudolph and Robert Altman from the play *Indians* by Arthur Kopit
PRODUCTION DESIGNER: Tony Masters
DIRECTOR OF PHOTOGRAPHY: Paul Lohmann
EDITORS: Peter Appleton and Dennis Hill
SOUND: William Sawyer and Richard Oswald
MUSIC: Richard Baskin
COSTUMES: Anthony Powell

PLOT SYNOPSIS:
1885. Fiction-writer Ned Buntline has turned William F. Cody into a legendary figure of the Wild West. In reality, the exploits of Buffalo Bill are pure fabrication. Cody trades on the tales in his successful show-business enterprise; 'Buffalo Bill's Wild West'. Cody is a sham; a hard-drinking womaniser whose famous tresses are a wig; even Annie Oakley is not the sharpest of shooters.

As a money-spinning coup for the first show of a new season Cody hires the services of Sitting Bull for fifty dollars a week. Initially Bull's interpreter, the strong, silent Halsey is mistaken for the great chief. Cody expects the insignificant frame of the real Sitting Bull to be booed and humiliated under the light of public scrutiny. He is proved wrong when Sitting Bull commands respect, stealing part of Cody's limelight.

When Sitting Bull and his troop go into the mountains to commune with the spirits they are thought to have escaped. Cody sets out in hot pursuit anticipating a glorious adventure. His inadequacies only highlight the chasm between the legend and the truth.

Sitting Bull returns, telling of a dream to perform before President Cleveland. It is a dream that comes true when the honeymooning Grover Cleveland requests a command performance. The event is a highpoint in the show's history.

When Cody and Buntline meet again they are irreconcilable. Buntline is off to preach in California. Soon afterwards Sitting Bull dies. Cody is left alone to ponder his life and live out the legend.

(Photo: Dino De Laurentis Productions)

COMMENT:

Fresh from the triumph of the Oscar-winning *Nashville* Robert Altman filmed his bustling, iconoclastic view of Buffalo Bill at the Stoney Indian Reservation in the Canadian Province of Alberta.

An audience expecting a rousing cowboys and Indians adventure, a not surprising assumption given the cast and the title, were severely disappointed. The film was a commercial failure.

'Burt Lancaster's elegantly rueful performance as Ned Buntline manages to give some contours to a flatly conceived rôle.'

Financial Times

'Burt Lancaster lends considerable charisma to his marginal but critical rôle as a myth maker.'

Monthly Film Bulletin

THE CASSANDRA CROSSING

(United Kingdom/USA 1976)
RUNNING TIME: 129 minutes

International Cine Productions

CAST: Sophia Loren (Jennifer), Richard Harris (Chamberlain), Ava Gardner (Nicole), Burt Lancaster (MacKenzie), Martin Sheen (Navarro), Ingrid Thulin (Elena), Lee Strasberg (Kaplan), John Phillip Law (Stack), Ann Turkel (Susan), O.J. Simpson (Father Haley), Lionel Stander (Conducter)

DIRECTOR: George Pan Cosmatos
PRODUCER: Carlo Ponti
SCREENPLAY: Robert Katz and George Pan Cosmatos with Tom Mankiewicz
PRODUCTION DESIGNER: Aurelio Crugnola
DIRECTOR OF PHOTOGRAPHY: Enio Guarniere
EDITOR: François Bonnot and Joe Pollini
SOUND: Carlo Palmiere
PRODUCTION MANAGERS: Cristina Luesch and Jean Pieuchot
MUSIC: Jerry Goldsmith
COSTUMES: Andriana Berselli

PLOT SYNOPSIS:

Three members of a Swedish Peace Group break into the International Health Organisation Headquarters in Geneva intent on planting an explosive device. An alarm is triggered and, following a chase through the bacteriological research area, one of the group is killed, one is injured and one escapes, infected with a rare pneumonic plague with no known antidote.

The plague carrier hides out on the Trans-Continental Express bound from Geneva to Stockholm. On board are internationally famous neuro-surgeon Jonathan Chamberlain and his ex-wife Jennifer; Nicole Hessler, wealthy wife of a German arms billionaire, who is accompanied by her pet bassett hound and her gigolo Navarro; black priest Father Haley, who is an undercover narcotics inspector, and aged entrepreneur Kaplan, a survivor of the Polish concentration camps.

In Geneva the authorities have placed Colonel Stephen MacKenzie in charge of the situation. He learns of the plague-carrier's presence on the train and decides that the entire unit must be quarantined. As no country in the West will allow the train to unload on their territory Mackenzie chooses to re-route the express to Yanov in Poland. This route entails crossing by the treacherous Cassandra bridge, disused since 1948 and almost certainly unable to carry the weight-load. MacKenzie is ordering 1000 passengers to their deaths.

Alerted to the danger of plague Chamberlain co-operates with MacKenzie, tending to the sick. An attempt to airlift the plague-carrier and Nicole's infected dog from the train is only partially successful and the dog is returned to Geneva for examination. In Nuremberg the train is sealed and, with forty-three security guards on board, journeys on to its inevitable fate in Poland. Miraculously the dog and many of the stricken passengers begin to recover; the liquid oxygen supply has counteracted the plague. With radio contact between the train and Geneva cut

(Photo: International Cine Productions)

MacKenzie refuses to stop the train despite evidence that the plague threat is over. Chamberlain and the other passengers take control of the train and, despite the loss of Navarro, Haley and Kaplan, uncouple several carriages before arriving at the bridge.

MacKenzie leaves his office believing all have perished. Chamberlain and many passengers have survived to tell the truth.

COMMENT:

Filmed on glamorous locations throughout Rome and Switzerland *The Cassandra Crossing* was part of a then highly popular series of disaster films involving spectacular mishaps and star names. *The Cassandra Crossing* was originally set to co-star Peter O'Toole and James Coburn but the star names were of little consequence to a film of fast-editing, action sequences and suspense.

A further commitment to Lew Grade Lancaster admits that this was one occasion where he was more concerned with the salary than the acting challenge. He has said; 'When I'm a papier mâché character I feel lost. I feel that if I'm not contributing anything to myself, who is the most important thing to contribute to, then I cannot make any other kind of contribution.'

'It is Lancaster's MacKenzie, duty-bound, solid, resolved and hating himself, who dominates the show.'

Films and Filming

VICTORY AT ENTEBBE

(USA 1976)

RUNNING TIME: 119 minutes

A David Wolper/Warner Brothers Production

CAST: Anthony Hopkins (Yitzhak Rabin), Burt Lancaster (Defence Minister Peres), Harris Yulin (Don Shomron), Stephen Geirasch (Mordechai Gur), Helmut Berger (Bose), Richard Dreyfuss (Netanyahu), Helen Hayes (Mrs Wise), Linda Blair (Chana), Elizabeth Taylor (Edra), Kirk Douglas (Herschel)

DIRECTOR: Marvin Chomsky
PRODUCER: Robert Guenette
ASSOCIATE PRODUCER: Albert J. Simon
SCREENPLAY: Ernest Kinoy
PRODUCTION DESIGNER: Edward Stephenson
DIRECTOR OF PHOTOGRAPHY: James Kilgore
EDITOR: Jim McElroy and Mike Gavaldon
SOUND: Larry Stevens
PRODUCTION MANAGER: Phillips Wylly
MUSIC: Charles Fox
COSTUMES: Jack Martell

PLOT SYNOPSIS:

Athens Airport, 27 June 1976. A group of Arab and German terrorists easily evade airport security checks and board the Air France flight to Paris. Taking control of the 'plane they land at Entebbe Airport in Uganda and issue an ultimatum that unless Israel and other countries free Arab guerrilla prisoners within four days then the hostages will be killed. Ugandan President Shomron shows little concern for the plight of the 250 passengers.

In Israel Prime Minister Rabin convenes his Cabinet and, through impassioned discussions with Defence Minister Peres, is resolute that the State of Israel will not negotiate with the terrorists. Rabin orders work to begin immediately on a rescue plan whilst apparently negotiating with the terrorist leader. In Entebbe, the hostages are divided into Jews and gentiles. One hostage, Mrs Wise, is removed to hospital never to be heard from again.

The terrorists release the non-Jewish hostages who provide invaluable information for the rescue mission leader Colonel Netanyahu. Israel announces it will discuss terms with the terrorists who make the concession of postponing their deadline of noon on Sunday, 1 July.

On the evening of 30 June, with Shomron out of the country at a convention in Mauritius, Netanyahu flies his troops to Entebbe and storms the airport. Three hostages, seven terrorists, twenty Ugandan soldiers and Netanyahu himself are killed but the remaining hostages are safely flown to Israel.

COMMENT:

After the successful Israeli rescue mission at Entebbe Airport during the summer of 1976 there was an unprecedented rush by film-makers to be the first on screen with a dramatisation of the events. Warner Brothers began immediate

(Photo: David Wolper/Warner Bros.) Anthony Hopkins

work on their version with Steve McQueen in the lead but scripting problems put them out of the race. Looking around to salvage their loss they arranged a co-production with David Wolper and thus *Victory at Entebbe* came into being.

Video-taped on hastily constructed studio sets in downtown Burbank, *Victory at Entebbe* was the first to reach British screens beating its nearest rival, *Raid on Entebbe*, by a week. Godfrey Cambridge died during filming and was replaced by Harris Yulin as the Idi Amin character Don Shomron.

In America both *Victory at Entebbe* and *Raid on Entebbe* were destined for television. The Israelis own film, and the best of the trio of productions which emerged, *Operation Thunderbolt*, appeared in 1977 with a largely Israeli cast.

'Burt Lancaster, Anthony Hoplkins and Richard Dreyfuss bring real conviction to the rôles of the Israeli top brass.'

Daily Mail

'Mr Lancaster lends a considerable authority. But since he last played Moses I imagine Mr Peres was a cakewalk.'

The Guardian

TWILIGHT'S LAST GLEAMING

(USA/Germany 1977)

RUNNING TIME: 146 minutes

A Geria Film Production, Lorimar-Bavaria Release

CAST: Burt Lancaster (Lawrence Dell), Richard Widmark (Martin Mackenzie), Charles Durning (President Stevens), Melvyn Douglas (Sec. of Defense), Paul Winfield (Powell), Burt Young (Garvas), Joseph Cotten (Sec. of State), Roscoe Lee Brown (James Forrest), William Smith (Hoxey), Richard Jaeckel (Capt. Towne)

DIRECTOR: Robert Aldrich
PRODUCER: Merv Adelson
EXECUTIVE PRODUCER: Helmut Jedele
SCREENPLAY: Ronald M. Cohen and Edward Huebsch from the novel *Viper Three* by Walter Wager
PRODUCTION DESIGNER: Rolf Zehetbauer
DIRECTOR OF PHOTOGRAPHY: Robert Hauser
EDITORS: Michael Luciano, Maury Winetrobe and William Martin
SOUND: James Willis
PRODUCTION SUPERVISOR: Henri Sokal
MUSIC: Jerry Goldsmith

PLOT SYNOPSIS:
16 November 1981. With the aid of three fellow convicts, Powell, Garvas and Hoxey, former Air Force General Lawrence Dell escapes from 'death row' in a Montana prison. Together they infiltrate an ICBM launch centre, blocking out all fail-safe systems and gaining the ability to launch nine nuclear missiles targeted on Russia. When the trigger-happy Hoxey kills two sergeants Dell shoots him dead for insubordination.

Dell lists his demands to the American President, David Stevens. He wants ten million dollars, transportation, the President as a hostage and the public disclosure of National Security Document 9759. The latter is lethal; explicitly stating the deception of the American people by the government in the Vietnam war. This demand is non-negotiable.

General Mackenzie believes Dell is bluffing. He persuades the President to implement Operation Gold whereby an Air Force team will enter the base on the blind side and plant a small nuclear device. However an alarm-system is triggered and, when Garvas is killed, Dell begins the countdown. Only a direct Presidential intervention averts disaster.

Stevens now agrees to the demands, aware that Dell cannot be allowed to succeed and that the authorities have positioned marksmen to shoot the renegades on sight. Stevens is considered expendable but secures a promise from his Secretary of Defense that a policy of open government will be followed and the contents of NSC 9759 disclosed on national television.

Exiting from the launch centre Dell and Powell are shot dead and Stevens is killed in the crossfire. Whether the Secretary of Defense will honour his pledge remains in doubt.

(Photo: Geria Film Production)

COMMENT:

With *Twilight's Last Gleaming* Lancaster set out to make a political film enveloped in a gripping action plot. However, the British distributors cut the film by twenty-six minutes, accentuating the action element and obfuscating the political intent.

In the full version the audience learns of the contents of the document which Lancaster's character is so desperate to make public. The document details a meeting between a former President, Foreign Secretary and Pentagon officials discussing America's involvement in Vietnam and concluding that America must have a deliberate policy of huge domestic casualties to prove that they mean business and will not be dictated to by mere bloodshed.

Filmed in Munich and Bavaria, *Twilight's Last Gleaming* was received poorly throughout the world and retitled *Nuclear Countdown* for a later video release.

'Lancaster, whether gleefully watching all his old military colleagues ranged against him or casually killing one of his own men who steps out of line handles the tricky rôle of Dell with aplomb.'

Films and Filming

THE ISLAND OF DR MOREAU

(USA 1977)

RUNNING TIME: 98 minutes

A Skip Steloff/Sandy Howard/Major Production

CAST: Burt Lancaster (Dr Moreau), Michael York (Braddock), Nigel Davenport (Montgomery), Barbara Carrera (Maria), Richard Baseheart (Sayer of the Law), Nick Cravat (M'Ling), The Great John L. (Boarman), Bob Ozman (Bullman), Fumio Demura (Hyenaman), Gary Baxley (Lionman), John Gillespie (Tigerman), David Cass (Bearman)

DIRECTOR: Don Taylor
PRODUCERS: John Temple-Smith and Skip Steloff
EXECUTIVE PRODUCERS: Samuel Z. Arkoff and Sandy Howard
SCREENPLAY: John Herman Shaner and Al Ramrus from the novel by H.G. Wells
PRODUCTION DESIGNER: Philip Jeffries
DIRECTOR OF PHOTOGRAPHY: Gerry Fisher and Ronnie Taylor
EDITOR: Marion Rothman
SOUND: David Hildyard
PRODUCTION MANAGER: John G. Wilson
MUSIC: Laurence Rosenthal
COSTUMES: Richard La Motte, Emma Porteus and Rita Woods

PLOT SYNOPSIS:
1911. After seventeen days adrift at sea two survivors of the shipwrecked liner *Lady Vain* are washed ashore on a remote Pacific island. Attacked by strange creatures one of the men disappears but the other, Andrew Braddock, reaches the sanctuary of a compound situated in a jungle clearing. The owner is a Dr Moreau, a man of science, conducting experiments on the island. Braddock is given the hospitality of the doctor until the arrival of the next ship, his companions are the hired mercenary Montgomery and the beautiful Maria. Braddock however, is advised never to leave the compound after dark.

Exploring the island Braddock catches sight of various creatures; half-man, half-beast in form. He demands an explanation from Moreau. Moreau tells of his breakthrough in genetic engineering and his varied success in turning animals into human beings, the process being unfortunately regressive. In a dank cave Braddock uncovers the results of eleven years of experimentation; mutants living by Moreau's laws that they must walk on all-fours, must never hunt man, nor spill blood. Disobedience is met by incarceration in the House of Pain. Revolted, Braddock bides his time, constructing a boat and trying to persuade Maria to leave with him.

When one of the creatures sheds blood disquiet grows and Braddock attempts to escape with Maria. The attempt is intercepted by Moreau who begins to experiment on Braddock, killing Montgomery when he tries to intervene. As Moreau has now shed blood the creatures rebel, killing Moreau and destroying the compound. Braddock and Maria flee the island to the safety of a passing vessel.

(Photo: Skip Steloff/Sandy Howard/Major Production)

COMMENT:

The Island of Dr Moreau was a remake of the 1933 *Island of Lost Souls* in which Charles Laughton had starred as H.G Wells' mad scientist. Filmed on the Virgin Islands by former actor turned director Don Taylor, the most striking feature was the make-up effects by John Chambers who had previously worked on *The Planet of the Apes* films.

'Lancaster, wisely playing the doctor very straight appears no more than slightly unbalanced.'

Evening News

'Dr Moreau is played by Burt Lancaster with the slow deliberation of gesture that he seems to adopt when he's not really interested.'

Sunday Telegraph

GO TELL THE SPARTANS

(USA 1978)

RUNNING TIME: 114 minutes

A Mar Vista Presentation of a Spartan Company Production

CAST: Burt Lancaster (Major Asa Barker), Craig Wasson (Cpl. Stephen Courcey), Jonathan Goldsmith (Sgt. Oleonowski), Marc Singer (Capt. Al Livetti), Joe Unger (Lt. Raymond Hamilton), Dennis Howard (Cpl. Abraham Lincoln), David Clennon (Lt. Finlay Wattsberg), Evan Kim (Cowboy), John Megna (Cpl. Ackley)

DIRECTOR: Ted Post
PRODUCER: Allan F. Bodoh and Mitchell Cannold
ASSOCIATE PRODUCER: Jesse Corallo
SCREENPLAY: Wendell Mayes from the novel *Incident at Muc Wa* by Daniel Ford
ART DIRECTOR: Jack Senter
DIRECTOR OF PHOTOGRAPHY: Harry Stradling Jr.
EDITOR: Millie Moore
SOUND: Bill Randall
PRODUCTION CO-ORDINATOR: Joel Westbrook
MUSIC: Dick Halligan
COSTUMES: Ron Dawson

PLOT SYNOPSIS:
   South Vietnam, 1964. Veteran Major Asa Barker, commanding an American Assistance Advisory Group at Penang, is ordered by his HQ to provide accurate information of the oupost of Muc Wa. He ignores the order and fabricates a report.
   Barker and his aide, Captain Olivetti, welcome the latest recruits – Corporal Courcey, who has been drafted; Lt. Hamilton, eager to prove himself; reserved medic Corporal Lincoln, and the war weary Sergeant Oleonowski who has served with Barker in Korea. Barker is ordered to occupy Muc Wa, a strategically important base once held by the French. Barker dispatches the new recruits along with South Vietnamese soldiers and mercenaries led by the bloodthirsty 'Cowboy'. The group digs in at Muc Wa with Oleonowski assuming command when Hamilton is stricken with dysentery. Nearby is a French cemetery with the inscription (from Herodotus),

Go tell the Spartans, thou that passeth by,
That here, obedient to their laws, we lie.

   Against the advice of Cowboy and Oleonowski, Courcey offers shelter to Vietnamese refugees. Hamilton is killed trying to rescue a colleague and Oleonowski, despairing of the situation, commits suicide. Barker sends Olivetti to take command whilst attempting to arrange air support. As the Vietcong offensive

144

(Photo: Spartan Company Production)

grows Barker is helicoptered into the area to evacuate his men. When Courcey refuses to leave the South Vietnamese behind Barker remains with him. Attempting to escape under cover of night all are killed except Courcey who vows to return home.

COMMENT:

Go Tell the Spartans had been around as a project for seven years and only went into production because of Lancaster's involvement. Reputedly he invested seventy-five thousand dollars of his own money in the production and received only a small fee for his acting services.

Before the film began he had been committed to the international adventure yarn The Wild Geese with Roger Moore and Richard Burton but pulled out when the opportunity arose to make something more significant.

Whilst reviews commented on the sensationalistic aspects of the film it was generally agreed that its heart was in the right place.

'The commanding presence of Burt Lancaster as a cigar-chomping Major fighting a battle for which he has no stomach lends a certain authority to the proceedings.'

Evening news

'Burt Lancaster plays Major Barker, an ageing professional soldier in charge of a group of military misfits who would be hard put to prevent a bunfight in a kindergarten.'

Daily Mirror

ZULU DAWN

(United Kingdom/South Africa 1979)
RUNNING TIME: 117 minutes

A Lamitas Presentation of a Samarkand Production

CAST: Burt Lancaster (Col. Durnford), Peter O'Toole (Lord Chelmsford), Simon Ward (William Vereker), John Mills (Sir Bartle Frere), Nigel Davenport (Col. Hamilton-Brown), Michael Jayston (Col. Crealock), Ronald Lacey (Norris Newman), Denholm Elliott (Lt. Col. Pulleine), Freddie Jones (Bishop Colenso), Christopher Cazenove (Lt. Coghill)

DIRECTOR: Douglas Hickox
PRODUCER: Nate Kohn
ASSOCIATE PRODUCER: Dieter Nobbe
SCREENPLAY: Cy Endfield and Anthony Storey
DIRECTOR OF PHOTOGRAPHY: Ousama Rawi
EDITOR: Malcolm Cooke
SOUND: Robin Gregory
PRODUCTION MANAGER: John Stodel
MUSIC: Elmer Bernstein
COSTUMES: Jon Jon Lambon

PLOT SYNOPSIS:
Africa, January 1879. It is decided that the British forces, led by Lord Chelmsford, will invade Zululand and strike a decisive blow in the war with the Zulus. The exercise has the air of the English at play; enjoying the sport of the battle and mindful of the reputations to be made. Chelmsford crosses the Buffalo River in contravention of previous agreements and an advance force under Lieutenant Colonel Pulleine is established at Isandhlwana.

A white Boer farmer chances upon the vast Impi army near Isandhlwana and reports his sighting. Chelmsford rejects his claims as fanciful; firm in his contention that a Zulu army lies massed to the east. One officer, one-armed Irish Colonel Durnford, believes that the threat is from the north – the Zulus want a quick, firm victory so that they can apply themselves to the crucial task of harvesting. Durnford has arrived with reinforcements from Natal in direct opposition to Chelmsford's orders. Chelmsford is unconvinced, berates Durnford for indiscipline and heads off for Ulundi in the east.

Shortly thereafter a scout for Durnford discovers the main Zulu force at Isandhlwana. In the ensuing battle the British troops are overwhelmed, Durnford, Pulleine and the force are massacred. Chelmsford's actions have ensured the worst defeat ever inflicted on a modern army by native troops.

COMMENT:
Filmed at Pietermaritzburg at Natal, *Zulu Dawn* was a prequel to the 1963 feature *Zulu* with a script by the original director Cy Endfield. Some twelve thousand extras were employed although controversy arose when it was discovered that the Zulus were being paid the equivalent of £1.50 per day.

(Photo: Samarkand Production) Peter O'Toole

During filming Lancaster told an interviewer; 'It makes a real change from some of the films being made today. I've turned down a lot of garbage lately. The bulk of films today are made for pure sensation. They lack originality and they don't have any kind of imagination.'

'Like too many epics *Zulu Dawn* boasts more box-office names than it can usefully employ and that includes O'Toole and Lancaster.'

Daily Mail

'A formidable British cast, aided by Burt Lancaster (sporting a rather ill-fitting Celtic accent as Durnford) does all it can for the tableauesque characters they are called on to play.'

The Observer

CATTLE ANNIE AND LITTLE BRITCHES

(USA 1980)
RUNNING TIME: 95 minutes

King-Hitzig Production for Monday films

CAST: Burt Lancaster (Bill Doolin), Rod Steiger (Tilghman), Amanda Plummer
(Annie), Diane Lane (Jenny), John Savage (Bittercreek Newcomb), Michael
Conrad (Engineer), Scott Glen (Bill Dalton), Redmond Gleeson (Red Buck),
William Russ (Little Dick Raidler), Buck Taylor (Dynamite Dick)

DIRECTOR: Lamont Johnson
PRODUCER: Rupert Hitzig and Alan King
ASSOCIATE PRODUCER: David Korda
PRODUCTION DESIGNER: Stan Jolley
DIRECTOR OF PHOTOGRAPHY: Larry Pizer
EDITOR: William Haugse
SOUND: Manuel Topete
PRODUCTION MANAGER: David Ball
MUSIC: Sanh Berti, Tom Slocum and Richard Greene
COSTUMES: Rita Riggs

PLOT SYNOPSIS:
In the dying days of the Old West the remnants of the Doolin-Dalton gang have
known better times. They continue an increasingly undistinguished career of
banditry, romanticised by the writer Ned Buntline and observed by two teenage
fans; Annie and Jenny.

When the gang rest up in a small town the orphan girls introduce themselves and
are entranced by a fantasy of outlaw life and by handsome half-breed Bittercreek
Newcomb. Warned of approaching lawmen the gang rides out. In relentless
pursuit is US Marshall Bill Tilghman.

The girls decide to join up with the gang, much to the displeasure of Bill Doolin,
but they soon ingratiate themselves and Doolin buoyed by their worship, attempts
to recapture the good old days. The gang decide to rob a bank but are discovered at
their half-way house by Tilghman. Only the quick thinking of Annie in stampeding
a herd of cattle allows the gang to escape. A second attempt at bank-robbing is
more successful until Tilghman and his men appear to arrest Doolin. Using a law-
officer as a hostage the gang escape but are dispirited by their recently desultory
attempts at banditry and determine to go their separate ways. Dalton considers
returning to politics in California and Doolin, old and tired, chooses to take a rest
cure at some hot springs.

At the hot springs Doolin is ambushed and arrested by Tilghman. Initially only
Annie and Jenny are willing to risk their lives to free Doolin. With Annie
disguised as a paper boy the two enter the jailhouse but are also apprehended by
Tilghman. However, Bittercreek Newcomb and other gang members ride to the
rescue, dynamiting the jail and freeing Doolin, Annie and Jenny. In a climactic
chase Jenny and Annie are arrested but the Doolin-Dalton gang evade capture
and ride onto the pages of the history books.

(Photo: King – Hitzig Production)

COMMENT:

Cattle Annie and Little Britches is the film that got away. Shot on a modest budget of just over five million dollars in Durango, Mexico, it suffered under the twin handicaps of being a Western, an unfashionable genre, and of having a distribution company with no faith in the film they had made.

The film was never given the chance to find its audience and only shown belatedly in New York during 1981 as a stop-gap replacement whilst the exhibitor awaited the arrival of the Sean Connery space drama *Outland*.

In Britain the film was never released in cinemas and went straight out on video.

'Lancaster has an easy tenderness that is never overdone. When he's by himself, naked, soaking at the hot springs, he's a magnificent sagging old buffalo. Lancaster looks happy in this movie and still looks tough; it's an unbeatable combination.'

New Yorker

'There are pleasant performances by Burt Lancaster, Rod Steiger, Diane Lane and Amanda Plummer.'

Voice

ATLANTIC CITY

(Canada/France 1980)
RUNNING TIME: 105 minutes

A Denis Heroux and John Kemeney Production
International Cinema Corporation and Selta Films

CAST: Burt Lancaster (Lou), Susan Sarandon (Sally), Kate Reid (Grace), Michael Piccoli (Joseph), Hollis McLaren (Chrissie), Robert Joy (Dave), Al Waxman (Alfie), Robert Goulet (Singer), Moses Znaimer (Felix), Agnes MacInnes (Vinnie)

DIRECTOR: Louis Malle
PRODUCER: Denis Heroux
EXECUTIVE PRODUCERS: Joseph Beaubain, Gabriel Boustany
ASSOCIATE PRODUCERS: Justine Heroux, Larry Nemsis
SCREENPLAY: John Guare
PRODUCTION DESIGNER: Anne Pritchard
DIRECTOR OF PHOTOGRAPHY: Richard Ciupka
EDITOR: Suzanne Baron
SOUND: Jean-Claude Laureux
PRODUCTION CO-ORDINATOR: Vincent Malle
MUSIC: Michel Legrand
COSTUMES: François Barbeau

PLOT SYNOPSIS:
Atlantic City, USA is a mix of old and new—a crumbling seaside resort being refurbished as the casino capital of the East. Sally, a waitress in an oyster bar and would-be croupier, lives in a rundown tenement. Each evening she washes herself with lemons to kill the smell of the fish, secretly observed by her neighbour Lou, a faded alleged mobster now playing nursemaid to Grace, who came to Atlantic City during the war for a Betty Grable look-alike contest and stayed.

Into their lives comes Dave, Sally's husband, and his pregnant girlfriend Chrissie, Sally's sister. They are on the run having stolen a consignment of dope in Philadelphia. Dave sets about selling the drugs using Lou as his messenger, however, when Dave is fatally stabbed Lou is left with the drugs and the money. This is his big break—he sells more of the dope, buys a new suit and pursues his notion of being a ladykiller. He impresses Sally with his wealth and poise but when Sally is attacked by the real mobsters he stands by helpless. He is revealed as a pathetic cowardly old man whose nostalgic tales of gangsterism were pure fantasy. When Sally is sacked from her job she successfully prevents Lou from fleeing the city. Eventually they are trapped by the two mobsters but Lou rises to the moment and shoots them both dead.

Childishly gleeful at his success—the first time he has killed anyone—he leaves town with Sally. The two book into a hotel and celebrate with champagne, sharing each other's dreams—Sally to deal her way to Monaco and Lou to show the boys from Florida that he made good. They spend the night together but Lou realises

150

(Photo: Denis Heroux/John Kemeney Production) Susan Sarandon

that he is an old man with a false past and allows Sally to leave with the money. He returns to Atlantic City and to Grace who sells the remainder of the drugs. They walk arm in arm together along the boardwalk perfectly suited.

COMMENT:
   Director Louis Malle passed over his first choice, Robert Mitchum, in favour of Lancaster for the part of ageing hood Lou. Mitchum, at sixty-three, wore his years too well to convince in the part. Lancaster, at sixty-seven, was ripe for it.
   The film proved a 'sleeper' in both the United States and Britain, virtually owing its discovery to successful screenings at world Film Festivals and an enthusiastic reception from the Press. The Los Angeles Film Critics voted it their Film of the Year awarding Lancaster Best Actor and John Guare Best Screenplay. The National Board of Review named their Best Film, Best Actor, Best Director and Best Screenplay Awards in favour of *Atlantic City, USA*. In the spring of 1982 the film was nominated for three Golden Globes and five Academy Awards without any wins. Lancaster, receiving his fourth nomination lost on the night to fellow veteran Henry Fonda for *On Golden Pond*. In Britain the film was nominated for four Academy Awards winning the Best Director for Louis Malle and Best Actor for Burt Lancaster. A genuinely surprised Lancaster was there, in person, to accept his award.

'Burt is marvellous. I'd not seen him in years, since Visconti's *Conversation Piece* . . . ah, yes, and *1900*, of course. He's marvellous! It's a great character and Burt loved it. Almost a caricature of himself, an old man pretending to be a big-time macho gangster. He was so enthusiastic! He has the reputation of being difficult but he was very easy and very much with us.'

Louis Malle, *Films Illustrated*, March 1981

THE SKIN

(Italy/France 1981)
RUNNING TIME: 131 minutes

Opera Film Produzione (Rome) – Gaumont SA (Paris)

CAST: Marcello Mastroianni (Curzio Malaparte), Burt Lancaster (General Mark Cork), Claudia Cardinale (Princess Consuelo Caracciolo), Ken Marshall (Jimmy Wren), Alexandra King (Deborah Wyatt), Carlo Giuffre (Eduardo Mazzullo), Yann Babilee (Jean-Louis), Jacques Sernas (General Guillaume)

DIRECTOR: Liliana Cavani
PRODUCER: Renzo Rosselini
EXECUTIVE PRODUCER: Manolo Bolognini
SCREENPLAY: Liliana Cavani and Robert Katz from the novel *The Skin* by Curzio Malaparte
ART DIRECTOR: Dante Ferretti
DIRECTOR OF PHOTOGRAPHY: Armando Nannuzzi
EDITOR: Ruggero Mastroianni
SOUND: Renato Marinelli
MUSIC: Lalo Schifrin
COSTUMES: Piero Tosi
ORIGINAL LANGUAGE TITLE: La Pelle

To date *The Skin* has not been shown in British Cinemas or made available for television. Filmed in Naples, Capri and the Cinecitta Studios in Rome, the film is set in the Naples of 1943 during the period of the Allied liberation. Ostensibly the plot deals with the clash of the two cultures. Lancaster plays General Clark who spearheads the Allied forces and dreams of taking the same route as the Caesars on their victorious return to Rome.

When the film was unveiled to the critics at the Cannes Film Festival, *The Times* said; 'her version of *La Pelle* is a vision of the Naples of 1943 as Sodom and Gomorrah, metamorphosing into the last days of Pompeii as Vesuvius erupts like a divine retribution. Against a background of every possible variety, physical and psychological, victors and vanquished share the mutual degradation.' The *Financial Times* claimed that Cavani's thesis was that 'all invasions are oppressive, whether by friendly or unfriendly forces' and that 'the plot sweeps up prostitution, child-labour, erupting volcanoes and veneral disease in its capricious but ever-more struggling arms.'

Reviewing the film from America the *Voice* said; 'Odious. How can anyone get so low? Probably by running headlong into an abyss of sensationalism and shock effect. Should *La Pelle* ever get distribution in America—and I hope it doesn't—don't see it on a full stomach or a full mind. You're guaranteed to lose both.'

The film was unavailable for viewing by the author.

Lancaster and director Bill Forsyth pictured during the making of *Local Hero*.

LOCAL HERO

(United Kingdom 1983)
RUNNING TIME: 111 minutes

An Enigma Production for Goldcrest

CAST: Burt Lancaster (Happer), Peter Reigert (Mac), Denis Lawson (Urquhart), Peter Capaldi (Oldsen), Fulton Mackay (Ben), Chris Rozycki (Victor), Jenny Seagrove (Marina), Jennifer Black (Stella), Chris Asante (Rev. Mac), Rikki Fulton (Geddes)

DIRECTOR: Bill Forsyth
PRODUCER: David Puttnam
ASSOCIATE PRODUCER: Iain Smith
SCREENPLAY: Bill Forsyth
PRODUCTION DESIGNER: Roger Murray-Leach
DIRECTOR OF PHOTOGRAPHY: Chris Menges
EDITOR: Michael Bradsell
SOUND: Louis Kramer
PRODUCTION MANAGER: Robin Douet
MUSIC: Mark Knopfler
COSTUMES: Penny Rose

PLOT SYNOPSIS:

Houston, Texas. Billionaire oil boss Felix Happer, head of Knox Oil and Gas, summons young executive MacIntyre to his penthouse. Mac is despatched to Scotland with the task of buying the picturesque coastal village of Ferness as the site for an oil refinery. Mac is also told to keep an eye on the skies as the study of the constellations is Happer's major obsession.

In Scotland MacIntyre is aided by the gauche Danny Oldsen and in Ferness must deal with local hotel proprietor Gordon Urquhart who doubles as the chief negotiator for the village. The villagers sense big money and as both Mac and Urquhart are skilful diplomats a deal seems imminent. Mac spends time getting to know the area and begins to question his big-city, rat-race values. He falls deeply in love with Stella, Urquhart's wife, whilst Danny pursues Marina, a marine biologist who might be a mermaid.

The negotiations reach an impasse when it is discovered that beachcomber Ben Knox owns the rights to the beach and will definitely not sell. Happer flies over to personally intervene – lured by Mac's glowing descriptions of the aurora borealis and shooting stars in the Ferness skies and as an escape from his analyst who has become almost as deranged as Happer.

In Ferness, Happer and Knox reach an understanding whereby the coastline will be used for research and study just as Marina has predicted all along. Mac returns to Houston unsuccessful in his business dealings but profoundly changed by his spell in Ferness.

154

(Photo: Enigma Production) Fulton Mackay

COMMENT:

Local Hero was filmed on a three million pound budget during the summer of 1982 in locations throughout Scotland and in Houston, Texas. The writer-director Bill Forsyth had completed the script with Lancaster in mind as the Texas oil billionaire Felix Happer, never dreaming that Lancaster would accept the part. Lancaster agreed to take the rôle solely on the strength of the script having seen neither of Forsyth's previous features, *That Sinking Feeling* (1979) or *Gregory's Girl* (1980),

Lancaster declared that it was the best script he had been offered since *Atlantic City* and welcomed Forsyth's sly sense of humour; 'Forsyth is a very perceptive person about human nature and frailties, and in his view everybody is a little strange, but he treats it all very gently with a very light humour. It's really refreshing to find someone who writes with such charming, lovely humour.'

'A charming and unusual comedy, Burt Lancaster's daffy millionaire is a hoot.'
Newsday

THE OSTERMAN WEEKEND

(USA 1983)

RUNNING TIME: 105 minutes

Osterman Weekend Productions, Inc.

CAST: Rutger Hauer (John Tanner), John Hurt (Fassett), Burt Lancaster (Maxwell Danforth), Meg Foster (Ali Tanner), Dennis Hopper (Dick Tremayne), Chris Sarandon (Joe Cardone), Craig T. Nelson (Bernie Osterman), Helen Shaver (Virginia Tremayne), Cassie Yates (Betty Cardone), Sandy McPeak (Stennings), Christopher Starr (Chris Tanner)

DIRECTOR: Sam Peckinpah
PRODUCER: Peter S. Davis and William N. Panzer
ASSOCIATE PRODUCER: Don Guest
SCREENPLAY: Alan Sharp from the novel by Robert Ludlum
DIRECTOR OF PHOTOGRAPHY: John Coquillon
EDITORS: David Rawlins and Ed Abroms

PLOT SYNOPSIS:

John Tanner, a brilliant, crusading journalist, seeks to interview the head of the CIA Maxwell Danforth on his TV show *Face to Face*.

Danforth is attracted to the idea as it provides an opportunity to exploit Tanner and break up a spy network called Omega. A CIA operative, Fassett, has uncovered the network and three of the agents involved are Tanner's close friends although they have kept their activities secret. The friends, Tanner, Cardone, Tremayne and Osterman, have an annual reunion called The Osterman Weekend. Danforth enlists Tanner's aid to reveal the spies during the forthcoming event, in return he agrees to appear on *Face to Face*.

Through various messages the three friends suspect they have been uncovered but decide to go ahead with the weekend. When Tanner's mistress is killed he attempts to flee with his wife and son but, following a kidnap attempt, is persuaded to remain at home under CIA surveillance. On the surface the weekend appears normal, the friends play water polo, watch movies and get drunk but tension grows as Fassett continues to manipulate the participants. When tempers explode and Osterman and Tanner confront each other they realise that the three friends have an illegal Swiss bank account in common and that is all; Fassett has gone mad and is using the situation to satisfy his bloodlust and exact revenge for Danforth murdering his wife. Tanner uses *Face to Face* to expose Danforth's methods and kills Fassett to protect his wife and child.

COMMENT:

Scheduled for an October 1983 release in America *The Osterman Weekend* marks the first time Lancaster has worked with veteran director Sam Peckinpah.

Based on the bestselling novel by Robert Ludlum, who received 100,000 dollars for the screen rights, *The Osterman Weekend* began filming on a budget of approximately ten million dollars during the middle of October 1982. The film was completed on schedule and on budget just before the end of the year. Most of

(Photo: Osterman Weekend Productions, Inc.)

the filming took place on the former estate of the late Robert Taylor whose property is now a working horse ranch situated between Beverly Hills and the Pacific Ocean in California.

Based on the appeal of Peckinpah and Ludlum, and the strength of the cast, the film was sold to 98 per cent of the world market six months before its public unveiling.

THE FUTURE

At the age of seventy Burt Lancaster finds himself in the enviable position of being a film star still very much in demand. Whilst many of his contemporaries are in semi-retirement or no longer command the calibre of rôle which they once earned Lancaster goes from strength to strength remaining as popular and active as he was in the 1950s. At the time of writing, *The Osterman Weekend* represents his most recent work for the cinema. Throughout 1983 his name has been linked to numerous projects. One film he didn't make was *Gorky Park*; the rôle he was interested in was played instead by William Hurt. Among the future films he has been announced for are; *The Crew*, a new work from the veteran Italian director Michelangelo Antonioni; *Kiss of the Spiderwoman*, to be directed by Hector Babenco from the novel by Manuel Puig, and *Maria's Lover* with the possible co-starring team of Nastassia Kinski and John Savage. For television Lancaster is due to join the large cast of a mini-series entitled *A.D.*, fellow luminaries in the show include Julie Christie and Irene Cara. With filming to take place in Tunisia, the series will be shown on the American NBC network during the 1984-85 season.

OTHER WORK

As mentioned in the main body of the text, Burt Lancaster has made guest appearances in the following films; *Variety Girl* (1947), *Three Sailors and a Girl* (1953), and *The List of Adrian Messenger* (1963). He has also been involved in the documentaries *King: A Filmed Record* (1970), a compilation on the life of Martin Luther King, and *The Cinema According to Bertolucci* (1975) which was made during the filming of *1900*. His other work, largely as a narrator, comprises *The Heart of Showbusiness* (1957), *Jenny is a Good Thing* (1969), *Ali the Fighter* (1975), *The Unknown War* (1978) and *Arthur Miller on Home Ground* (1979).

His stage work has been *The Sound of Hunting* (1945) on Broadway, *Knickerbocker Holiday* (1971) in San Francisco and a play about Huckleberry Finn and Tom Sawyer with Kirk Douglas in Los Angeles in 1981.

On television he has appeared in *Moses* and *Victory at Entebbe*, both discussed in the main text. In 1977 he acted as the host for a special, *Psychic Phenomenon: Exploring the Unknown*. In 1981 he returned to film in Italy, playing the medieval Pope Gregory X in a spectacular version of *Marco Polo*. He attempted to interest the American networks in a television version of the play *Going Gently* about two terminal cancer patients but to no avail. The material was considered too risky for primetime viewing despite the projected casting of Lancaster and Art Carney.

INDEX